Cavapoos

The Owner's Guide from Puppy to Old Age

Choosing, Caring for, Grooming, Health, Training and Understanding Your Cavapoo Dog

By Morgan Andrews

Copyright and Trademarks

Disclaimer and Legal Notice

of any information presented in this work. This publication is designed to provide information in regard to the subject matter covered. Neither the author nor the publisher assume any responsibility for any errors or omissions, nor do they represent or warrant that the ideas, information, actions, plans, suggestions contained in this book are in all cases accurate. It is the reader's responsibility to find advice before putting anything written in this book into practice. The information in this book is not intended to serve as legal advice.

Photo Credit: Christy Shanklin of Christy's Puppies

Foreword

Many of the world's top breeders have been involved in contributing to this book, and once you've read the book, you will have all the information you need to make a well-informed decision about whether or not the Cavapoo is the breed for you.

As an expert trainer and professional dog whisperer, I would like to teach you the human side of the equation, so you can learn how to think more like your dog and eliminate behavioral problems with your pet.

If you're like I am and encounter many dogs in your daily life, you may suddenly be hearing the words "hybrid" or "designer" dogs frequently.

The Cavapoo is a crossbreed that combines the Cavalier King Charles Spaniel and Miniature or Toy Poodle.

Cavapoos live up to the hybrid expectation. They are known for their friendly and outgoing personality, which makes them great family pets. They are also cuddly and social dogs that need lots of attention.

While Cavapoos can make excellent companions, it is important to understand the advantages, disadvantages and potential health problems of both Cavaliers and Poodles before buying.

The information in this book will help you to form a fuller sense of what life with a Cavapoo would be like and arm you with the correct questions to ask in your discussions with breeders.

Acknowledgments

In writing this book, I also sought tips, advice, photos and opinions from many experts of the Cavapoo breed.

In particular I wish to thank the following wonderful experts for going out of their way to help and contribute:

COPY-EDITING

Special thanks to Danna Colman

CAVAPOO BREEDERS - USA & CANADA

Rebecca Posten of Riverside Puppies
http://www.riversidepuppies.biz

Laura Koch of Petit Jean Puppies
https://www.petitjeanpuppies.com

Christy Shanklin of Christy's Puppies
http://www.cpuppies.com/

Dena Fidanza of Dena's Doggies
http://www.denasdoggies.com

Windie Sturges of Calla Lily Cavapoo
http://www.callalilycavapoo.com

Cindi Stump of Stump Farm Puppies Too
http://www.stumpfarmpuppiestoo.com

Jim and Johanna Abernathy and Terri Schnieders of Willowbrook Cavaliers
http://www.willowbrookcavaliers.com/

Eva Chamberlin of Cee Cee's Puppy Palace
http://www.ceeceespuppypalace.com/

Phyllis Oliver of Dobralco Silky Terriers
http://www.dobralcosilkyterriers.com

Jackie Arana of My Cavapoos
http://www.mycavapoos.com

Amy Dillabough of A & R Country Kennel
http://www.arcountrykennel.com

CAVAPOO BREEDERS - UNITED KINGDOM

Kirstin Pollington of Milky Paws
http://www.milkypaws.co.uk

Charlotte Purkiss of Lotties Cavapoos
http://www.lottiescavapoos.co.uk/

PHOTOGRAPHY FROM CAVAPOO OWNERS

Nicki Mannix owner of Bella
Louise Driscoll owner of Walter
Dawn Smith owner of Dughie-Doo
Paul & Michele Flower owner of Wally
Charlotte G Photography - Charlotte Gravatt (owner of Honey)
Helen Wilson owner of Ralph
Danna Colman owner of Georgia

Table of Contents

Table of Contents

Table of Contents

Table of Contents

Table of Contents

Table of Contents

Chapter 1 – What Are Cavapoos?

The Cavapoo is one of the oldest "designer" crossbreeds. Cavapoos were first bred in the USA during the 1950s with the goal of creating a friendly, non-shedding dog that didn't suffer from the genetic conditions associated with Cavaliers.

It wasn't until the 1980s that crossbreed dogs – or hybrids – started to become a popular alternative to purebreds.

Photo Credit: Nicki Mannix owner of Bella

Crossbreeds that are half Poodle, such as Labradoodles and Cockapoos, have become particularly common due to the Poodle's intelligence and non-shedding coat. The Cavapoo is bred around the world but is especially popular in countries such as the UK and Australia (the breed is called the Cavoodle in Australia).

The Cavapoo has not been selectively bred for its appearance, which is why it's considered a crossbreed. This also means that it's not possible to guarantee a Cavapoo puppy will inherit the desired characteristics of the parent breeds. Even so, the Cavapoo is usually a lovely dog with a friendly, confident personality.

Dedicated Cavapoo breeders are working hard to improve the genetics of the hybridization so that the dogs breed true, reliably passing on their best characteristics to the next generation.

Although some hybridizations are nothing more than poorly considered "designer dogs," the Cavapoo mix is an excellent combination of two hardy breeds and will undoubtedly gain independent recognition by the various canine governing organizations in the years to come.

We asked Terri Schnieders of Willowbrook Cavaliers what she thought made Cavapoos special: "Cavapoos are an amazing breed. Super-smart, affectionate and loyal. They are your best couch buddy or are also very capable of taking a swim, run or hike. Wherever you are is where they are most happy."

The Two Breeds: Cavalier King Charles Spaniel and Miniature or Toy Poodle

When choosing any crossbreed, make sure you understand the characteristics and temperament of both parent breeds. It's impossible to guess which characteristics a Cavapoo will inherit as there is always an element of luck. This applies to both the dog's behavior and physical attributes – including health problems.

Overview of the Cavalier King Charles Spaniel

Cavalier King Charles Spaniels are friendly dogs that love being around humans. The Cavalier is a toy dog (a term that traditionally refers to a very small dog or a grouping of small breeds of dog) that is popular around the world due to its affectionate and friendly nature. This friendliness also means that the Cavalier requires lots of attention and human interaction – which is why many Cavapoos have the same requirements.

History

The Cavalier King Charles Spaniel can be traced back to 16th century England. Toy Spaniels were popular amongst ladies of the court, but it wasn't until later that the dogs were officially called King Charles Spaniels. This name was due to King Charles II owning several Toy Spaniels. At this time, the lack of a breed standard meant that the dogs varied greatly in appearance.

The breed standard we know today was created in 1928. This was also when the name "Cavalier King Charles Spaniel" became official. The breed standard hasn't changed much since 1928, but the breed's popularity has increased dramatically – especially in the UK.

Temperament

There are few breeds that can match the unassuming friendliness of the Cavalier King Charles Spaniel. Cavaliers seem to love everybody and always want a stroke or cuddle from strangers. This makes them excellent family pets, but poor guard dogs.

Cavaliers are intelligent dogs that are happy to please; however, they do have a "mind of their own," as many Cavalier owners will attest! This means they need to be properly trained using positive reinforcement techniques to avoid developing bad behaviors such as ignoring commands.

Many people think that Cavaliers are quiet dogs. This is not always the case. While some Cavaliers won't bark even if an intruder enters the home, others love nothing more than to bark manically at the smallest noise. A parent Cavalier with a barking tendency often passes this trait down to its offspring. If possible, spend some time with the Cavalier parent before adopting a Cavapoo to see whether it's prone to barking.

Cavaliers are companion dogs that are happiest when spending time with humans and other dogs. They shouldn't be left in kennels or by themselves for long periods of time and need plenty of attention. The dogs do, however, make great apartment pets provided they get daily exercise.

Physical Appearance

Cavaliers are small dogs. They typically grow to around 30cm-35cm (11.81 inches - 13.77 inches) in height and weigh up to 8kg (17.63 lbs). The color of Cavaliers varies, with Blenheim, black/tan and tricolor amongst the most common.

Health

Unfortunately, the selective breeding of Cavaliers has led to the development of a number of hereditary health problems. These include Mitral Valve Disease – a serious condition that can cause death or epilepsy – and a condition affecting the spine called Syringomyelia.

These are serious conditions that can cause widespread pain and early death. Mitral Valve Disease, in particular, is of increasing concern amongst Cavalier breeders. It's a disease that affects nearly all purebred Cavaliers by the time they reach ten years old although MVD can be managed with medication.

For this reason, top breeders of Cavaliers should provide proof that a puppy has healthy parents.

The Cavalier's health problems are one of the reasons why the Cavapoo is becoming more popular. F1 Cavapoos, which are the direct offspring of a Cavalier, are thought to be less likely to suffer from the breed's genetic conditions; although, there is still debate about whether hybrid dogs are less likely to suffer from genetic conditions. Whether designer puppies are healthier or not, there is always a chance that a Cavapoo will inherit genetic conditions.

Overview of Miniature and Toy Poodles

The Cavapoo can be bred using either a Miniature or Toy Poodle. These breed variants are similar, but there are some important differences.

History

Poodles are thought to be one of the oldest breeds of dog that are still around today. The breed was originally developed in Germany but became popular as a water retriever in France. While Standard Poodles are the oldest variant, Toy and Miniature followed soon after.

Temperament

Poodles are among the most clever of dog breeds, with only the Border Collie outranking the breed in intelligence tests. This is the reason the Cavapoo is often fast and easy to train.

This intelligence can sometimes come at a cost. For example, if a Poodle thinks it's the pack leader, it may not respond to commands. Poodles need a strong owner and proper training using positive techniques to prevent this stubbornness from developing. They also need regular mental stimulation, as their intelligence makes it easy for them to become bored.

Despite their regal appearance, Poodles can be quite entertaining with their fun personalities. While Poodles love to show affection to their owners, they are often unfriendly with strangers – at least until they get to know them. They are rarely aggressive but may growl or become snappy when annoyed or scared.

When choosing a Cavapoo, make sure you know whether it is the offspring of a Toy or Miniature Poodle. Both options can make fantastic pets, but there are some important differences in behavior.

The Toy Poodle is extremely loyal to its owner. With proper training, Toy Poodles can be excellent family pets. However, if the breed isn't trained correctly, it is prone to negative behaviors such as biting and growling.

Miniature Poodles are considered more playful than Toy Poodles; although, there is always variation depending on the dog's character. Miniature Poodles are also often more patient, making them better suited to family life. For this reason, some Cavapoo owners specifically look for puppies that have been bred from a Miniature Poodle.

Physical Appearance

The Toy Poodle is slightly smaller than the Miniature. Toy Poodles often grow to a height around 10 inches (25.4 cm), while Miniature Poodles stand at approximately 15 inches (38.1 cm).

Health

Like other purebreds, both Toy and Miniature Poodles are likely to suffer from genetic conditions. Addison's disease, thyroid problems, hip dysplasia and epilepsy are some of the most commonly reported conditions.

Many Poodles also suffer from patellar luxation. This is when the kneecap doesn't sit properly in the patellar groove, causing it to "pop out" when the dog's knee is flexed. This can cause temporary lameness. While the severity of patellar luxation varies, it can eventually lead to difficulty walking.

Poodles are also more likely to suffer from ear infections than other dogs.

Physical Characteristics of the Cavapoo

It's hard not to fall for the irresistible cuteness of a Cavapoo.
When you first visit a litter of puppies, there is a strong chance
you'll fall in love. Consider yourself warned!

The Cavapoo is a crossbreed, which means there isn't a defined
breed standard. The size of a Cavapoo partly depends on
whether a Toy or Miniature Poodle was used. There are typically
two size classifications:

A Toy Cavapoo will be approximately 11-14 inches (27.94 - 35.46
cm) in height and weigh approx 7-10 kg (15.43 - 22.04 lbs).

A Miniature Cavapoo is approximately 13-16 inches (33.02 - 40.64
cm) in height and weigh an average of 11-15 kg (24.25 - 33.06 lbs).

The Cavapoo has beautiful floppy ears. Many people love the
ears of the Cavapoo as it provides a permanent puppy-like
appearance. Other characteristics include a soft coat and compact
body.

It is very common for Cavapoos to have amazing and
exceptionally long eye lashes, which on average can be a good
1.5 inches long.

Cavapoos are agile dogs that love to run and explore. This agility
combined with the breed's excitable nature can make them a
handful as puppies. The Cavapoo is also not a dog that can be
easily kept off the sofa!

The Cavapoo is sometimes described as hypoallergenic. While
there is little evidence that a truly hypoallergenic dog exists,
many people with dog allergies find that Poodle crossbreeds
don't cause much of a reaction. A Cavapoo may also inherit the

non-shedding genes of the Poodle; although, this can't be guaranteed. Windie Sturges of Calla Lily Cavapoo adds: "The curl gene and the non-shed gene are two totally separate genes. So you can have a low-shed or no-shed with a wavy coat and the same 50/50 possibility with the flat coat."

The overall appearance of a Cavapoo depends on which parent provides the dominant genes. Some have a distinctive Cavalier appearance, while others more closely resemble Poodles. It can sometimes be difficult to guess the eventual appearance of a Cavapoo as a puppy. The coat can be soft, curly, long or wavy.

Coat Colors

Cavapoos can have a number of different colors. Some of the most common include black white, red (ruby), Blenheim (white and red), tricolor, apricot, cream and gold. The coat can either be one solid color or be made up of various complex markings. Some of the rarer colors available are sable, chocolate brown (with liver nose and hazel eyes) and merle.

Louise Driscoll, owner of Walter, has this experience: "Most Cavapoo owners experience a big change in colour in their dog's coats as they mature. Walter was very much 'Apricot' (Ginger) and now so very light. This also occurs in the darker ones, too."

Health and Lifespan

The lifespan of a Cavapoo can vary greatly depending on whether any genetic conditions are inherited. A healthy Cavapoo often lives to around 10-15 years. Some of the healthiest Cavapoos have been known to live up to 20 years.

Talk to your breeder about the average lifespan of their dogs and what you might expect.

Cavapoos, just like any designer dog, can potentially suffer from genetic health conditions. Just because a dog is a crossbreed doesn't mean that it won't be affected by genetic problems. If a breeder tells you that Cavapoos don't suffer from health problems, you should leave as quickly as possible! Reputable breeders never make this claim and will be happy to discuss the breed's health issues.

A Cavapoo can develop the health conditions associated with either the Cavalier or Poodle. For this reason, the breeder should be able to prove that the parent dogs have been checked for the most common conditions.

Don't be satisfied by a breeder that tells you the parent dogs have been "checked by vets." Many genetic conditions don't appear until later in life and cannot be detected without proper testing. Ask for written documentation of any tests the parents have had before you buy.

What Are F1, F2, and F1b?

Crossbreed dogs are labeled according to their generation. The most common labels are:

F1 – An F1 Cavapoo is when a purebred Cavalier King Charles Spaniel is crossed with a purebred Toy or Miniature Poodle. This is the most common crossbreed and usually has the greatest vigor.

F1b – If a Cavapoo is bred back with a Poodle, this is called F1b. F1b Cavapoos are most likely to have a non-shedding coat.

F2 – An F2 Cavapoo is when two Cavapoos are bred together. These dogs tend to have less vigor. The advantage is that the breeder has more control over which attributes are selected.

F3 – If two F2 Cavapoo dogs are used for a litter, the puppies are labeled as F3. This continues for each further generation.

What Can You Expect From a Cavapoo Puppy?

Get ready for a wild ride when you bring your Cavapoo puppy home! Cavapoos typically can't wait to start exploring their environment and are naturally curious. They are lovable dogs that quickly become part of the family.

The First Few Days

Like any puppy, a Cavapoo will take some time to get used to its new surroundings. Once settled in, the puppy is likely to be inquisitive and eager to discover every corner of its new home. It's important to fully puppy-proof your home so that your new dog can satisfy its curiosity safely.

You should be prepared for crying and barking during the first few nights. The Cavapoo can be a surprisingly vocal breed considering its small size. Make sure you have a plan for how to deal with crying before you bring your puppy home so that you can be consistent.

Some breeders recommend keeping the dog in a crate next to your bed for the first few nights, while others say that the dog should be kept downstairs from day one. The most important thing is to pick a tactic and stick to it.

Dealing with Excitable Behavior

Cavapoos love attention, especially as puppies, and often demand it by barking and being excitable. The puppy's cute appearance can make it irresistible, especially for visitors and children. This is understandable, but it's important to remember that behaviors rewarded as a puppy are likely to continue as the dog gets older. It's also a good idea to train a Cavapoo puppy to be left alone from a young age to prevent social anxiety.

The sweet "ball of fluff" appearance of Cavapoos often means friends and families can't wait to meet them. This makes it easy to socialize the puppy with humans. Cavapoos are naturally friendly and usually aren't aggressive, but socialization is always important.

Photo Credit: Nicki Mannix owner of Bella

Be aware that the constant excitement of meeting new people can potentially lead to behavioral problems. Many people's natural reaction when interacting with a Cavapoo puppy is to squeal with delight and pet, hug and pick up the dog. This isn't a bad thing but can teach a puppy that humans always provide excitement. While over-excited greetings may not be an issue for all dogs, it's a good idea to ask visitors to be calm when they first meet a Cavapoo puppy.

Preventing Bad Habits

Cavapoos are usually intelligent, fast-learning dogs. This is great for training them as puppies but also means you need to be careful about accidentally reinforcing unwanted behaviors.

The Cavapoo likes to explore with its mouth, which is "dog speak" for saying that they bite a lot as puppies! The biting is rarely aggressive but can still be painful and should be discouraged from a young age. If you don't train your Cavapoo to understand that biting isn't acceptable, it can become a habit later in life.

For this reason, it's important that all of your family understands how to react to play biting. There are a number of different methods – yelping when the dog bites you and ignoring him are two examples, but consistency is of utmost importance. As long as you are consistent, play biting should gradually decrease as the puppy realizes it's not the way to get attention or play.

Potty training is usually relatively quick with a Cavapoo puppy. The Cavapoo is an intelligent breed that will start to understand quickly if you are consistent. However, this doesn't mean potty training is instant, as it can still take up to six months for a Cavapoo to be fully trustworthy in the house.

Cavapoo Personality and Temperament

Cavapoos are smart and well-natured dogs. They often have a strong personality that makes them instantly lovable. Most Cavapoos love being around people and are happy as long as they have company. This also means that they need to be properly trained to prevent separation anxiety, especially if they are the only dog in the house.

The Cavapoo is an affectionate breed that quickly learns to love every member of the family. While they may bond more strongly with one member of the family, they are always happy to see a friendly face. Whenever a family member arrives home, you can expect to see the Cavapoo running to greet them with a furiously wagging tail.

Cavapoos can sometimes be tiring dogs due to their high energy levels. This is a trait that varies depending on the dog's genetics and training. Some Cavapoos are laid back and easygoing, while others are naturally excitable.

While the Cavapoo may bark when it hears noises, it is not usually a good choice for a guard dog. A Cavapoo is more likely to lick an intruder than alert you to his or her presence!

There are exceptions depending on which genes are inherited. Poodles often make good watchdogs, so these traits may be inherited, although this can't be relied upon.

Physical and Mental Requirements

The Cavapoo needs regular daily exercise. The small size of the crossbreed means that some of this can take place indoors. A game of tug of war, fetch or other stimulating activity such as swimming can provide both mental and physical exercise.

The Cavapoo needs a walk every day. A single long walk each day, along with the occasional playtime, should be plenty to keep the dog happy and reduce the chances of destructive behavior. Two twenty-minute walks are also enough for most Cavapoos, although some need more exercise.

Aside from physical exercise, it is vital for a Cavapoo to be provided with mental stimulation. Many behavioral problems with Cavapoos can be traced back to either a lack of exercise or mental stimulation. Barking, whining and chewing furniture can all be a sign of boredom.

Any activity that causes the dog to think can prevent boredom. Games involving finding treats can be particularly fun for Cavapoos. Mental stimulation also means that the dog will be sleepy and less destructive, which can be a relief if you own a lively Cavapoo!

Socializing a Cavapoo

The Cavapoo is often an easy dog to socialize. They are naturally inquisitive and love meeting new people and other dogs. If a Cavapoo is gradually exposed to more situations during the socialization period, it is likely to grow up to be a confident and outgoing dog.

The socialization period for a Cavapoo is usually between the age of three to twelve weeks. This is when it's most important for the puppy to meet different people, socialize with other dogs and have new experiences. The best breeders will do some basic socialization before you adopt the dog.

Depending on when you adopt a Cavapoo, you may only have a few short weeks to socialize the puppy. Make sure you have a plan for socialization before you adopt, so you don't waste any of the precious socialization period. If possible, take your puppy to socialization groups.

Does It Matter That Cavapoos Are a Crossbreed?

Without getting into the "politics" of hybrid dogs, the main thing you should know is that not everyone believes in the benefits of crossbreeds. While it's important to thoroughly research any dog before you adopt, don't let other people's opinions and biases affect your decision.

There are some breeders who feel that crossbreeds are a "scam" as they cost as much – or sometimes more – as purebreds without the selectively bred traits. These breeders also don't believe that crossbreeds are healthier than purebreds. Even so, many people find that crossbreeds have more vigor than purebreds and are also less likely to show extreme behaviors.

It's vital to understand the possible traits and characteristics of a puppy before you buy. While a Cavapoo is ideally bred for the Poodle's intelligence and non-shedding coat and the Cavalier's friendly attitude, there is no guarantee that these traits will be passed on. It's equally likely that a puppy will receive the undesirable traits of both parent breeds. The genetic characteristics of a crossbreed are essentially a random mix between the two parents.

The appearance of a Cavapoo can also vary. Some Cavapoos mature to look like one of the parents rather than a mixture of both. The size of the breed can also differ. It's common for a hybrid dog to be adopted because of its cute appearance, only to grow up to look completely different.

In short, the Cavapoo is often a lovable and social pet, but there are no guarantees as to which traits will be passed on. There is always a risk when choosing any dog, including purebreds. You should try to choose a breed or crossbreed that is most likely to match your requirements and lifestyle.

Breeder Eva Chamberlin of Cee Cee's Puppy Palace comments: "Cavapoos are the best of the hybrids. I have had repeat buyers of their second and third puppies. Cavapoos are cuddly, playful, smart and are very adaptable to their owners lifestyle. I have dogs that are therapy dogs for various issues, diabetes, hospital, seizure detection etc. Some of them go to hospitals and lay on the beds with sick people. They train easily and can acclimate to apartments, beaches and boats."

The Cavapoo and Children

The Cavapoo often makes an excellent family pet and is usually tolerant of children. The adorable appearance, loyal nature and affectionate behavior of the Cavapoo make them easy for children to love.

Sometimes a Cavapoo can be too energetic and boisterous for children, but this behavior often settles down as the dog gets older. It's also important to socialize a Cavapoo puppy with people of different ages including babies, toddlers and young children.

Like all dog breeds, the Cavapoo should be supervised when around young children. This is to ensure the safety of both the dog and the child. In many cases, accidents happen when a child doesn't understand how to treat a dog with respect.

The Cavapoo and Other Animals

A dog's behavior around other animals is largely dependent on how well it was socialized as a young puppy. By properly socializing your puppy with a variety of different animals, including as many other dogs as possible, your dog will learn proper manners and also won't be scared as an adult.

Cavapoos are usually playful and curious around other dogs. This makes the breed easy to socialize; although, their energetic nature may annoy other dogs until they learn to read body language. Shyness around other dogs usually only becomes a problem if a Cavapoo hasn't been socialized properly.

Photo Credit: Paul & Michele Flower owner of Wally

Cavapoos love to chase, so it's important to keep them in enclosed areas. If a fence doesn't surround the garden, the dog is likely to chase squirrels, birds and other small animals. This could potentially lead the dog to run into a road or other dangerous situation without realizing.

Is There a Difference Between Male and Female Cavapoos?

There is a common misconception that male Cavapoos – or male dogs in general – don't make good pets. This usually isn't true! In most cases, there is little difference between male and female Cavapoos as long as the dog is neutered or spayed by the time it reaches 6-8 months old.

The primary reason cited for not wanting a male dog is spraying and urine marking. Neutering your Cavapoo has health benefits. The surgery decreases hormone levels. It puts an end to territorial urine marking in males and solves the issue of moodiness in females in heat.

If the dog isn't neutered or spayed, breeders have reported several differences between male and female dogs. Male Cavapoos tend to mature slower and are also more relaxed. Female Cavapoos are faster to mature and are typically more confident and outgoing.

While there might be some differences in behavior between unaltered male and female Cavapoos, the gender doesn't have a major impact. The personality of the dog and the training it receives will affect the dog's behavior much more than gender.

One or Two?

When you are sitting on the floor surrounded by puppies, taking two home seems like a great idea. Pause, take a breath, and think again. Adopting a single dog is a huge commitment. You are pledging your time and money to a living creature.

With the second dog, all of that doubles. Cavapoos require positive training and socialization to be good pets. If you've never owned the breed before, start slow. You need to really be certain that a Cavapoo is "the" dog for you before taking on the responsibility of caring for more than one.

Is It Best to Buy a Cavapoo Puppy or Adult?

Deciding whether to buy an adult or puppy is a difficult choice. There are advantages to both, so the decision mainly comes down to your personal preference.

Here are some considerations when deciding whether to buy a puppy or adult:

• Puppies are a lot of fun but are also hard work! Aside from potty training and socialization, puppies can also be destructive around the house. This is especially true for Cavapoo puppies that often become fluffy bundles of energy at around eight or nine weeks old.

• Puppies need constant care and can't be left on their own for more than 2-3 hours. If you have a full-time job, buying an adult dog that can be left for longer may be a better option.

• It's difficult to judge the character of a puppy at adoption age. A dog's personality hasn't fully formed at 8-12 weeks, and it can take time for the true personality to become apparent. If you adopt an adult dog, you can quickly judge its personality and temperament.

• The immature stage of a dog's life lasts a lot longer than most people think. Dogs don't finish adolescence until they are around 18 months old for smaller dogs and up to 3 years for larger breeds. Adolescence can be a difficult time for a dog owner, as the dog is likely to be less obedient, boisterous and require more exercise.

• When adopting an adult dog, you don't have to worry about house training and socialization. This makes adult dogs far less time consuming and stressful, especially during the first few months.

• Adopting an adult dog is often cheaper. Cavapoo puppies can cost more than $1000 depending on the breeder.

• On the other hand, if you buy a puppy you have full control over the dog's upbringing and socialization. This is important, especially if you have children, as there is no guarantee that an adult dog was properly socialized as a puppy.

• When buying a puppy, you also don't have to worry about bad habits established by the previous owner.

It is sometimes difficult to find an adult Cavapoo for adoption. Dogs of all breeds need new homes regularly, however, so if you keep looking you'll almost certainly find one. Once you find a Cavapoo for adoption, make sure you visit and spend time with the dog before making a decision.

A Cavapoo surrendered for adoption will, however, possibly have behavior issues. Find out in advance exactly why the dog was given up. In the best case scenario, it may simply be an instance of the previous owner no longer being able to care for the dog. If, however, there was a problem, make sure it's one with which you can cope before taking the dog home.

Even if you don't decide to adopt a dog (of any breed) under rescue circumstances, please support the work of these invaluable organizations with your donations or volunteer hours. These groups are constantly in need, and they perform a vital service, literally saving thousands of canine lives every year.

Chapter 2 – Cavapoo Dog Breed Standard

A breed standard is created to codify all the best traits of a breed to provide a basis by which exceptional examples of the dog may be judged in competition and for breeding purposes.

Since the Cavapoo is not an official breed, the following are the standards for the parent breeds. This will give you some idea of the traits and look of the Cavapoo based on the two foundation breeds.

The American Kennel Club (AKC) standards are produced verbatim. The only changes incorporated are typographical to enhance readability.

AKC Standard for the Cavalier King Charles Spaniel:

General Appearance: The Cavalier King Charles Spaniel is an active, graceful, well-balanced toy spaniel, very gay and free in action; fearless and sporting in character, yet at the same time gentle and affectionate. It is this typical gay temperament, combined with true elegance and royal appearance, which are of paramount importance in the breed. Natural appearance with no trimming, sculpting or artificial alteration is essential to breed type.

Size, Proportion, Substance: Size - Height 12 to 13 inches at the withers; weight proportionate to height, between 13 and 18 pounds. A small, well-balanced dog within these weights is desirable, but these are ideal heights and weights and slight variations are permissible. **Proportion** - The body approaches squareness, yet if measured from point of shoulder to point of buttock, is slightly longer than the height at the withers. The height from the withers to the elbow is approximately equal to the height from the elbow to the ground. **Substance** - Bone moderate in proportion to size. Weedy and coarse specimens are to be equally penalized.

Head: Proportionate to size of dog, appearing neither too large nor too small for the body. **Expression** - The sweet, gentle, melting expression is an important breed characteristic. **Eyes** - Large, round, but not prominent and set well apart; color a warm, very dark brown; giving a lustrous, limpid look. Rims dark. There should be cushioning under the eyes, which contributes to the soft expression. Faults - small, almond-shaped, prominent, or light eyes; white surrounding ring. **Ears** - Set high, but not close, on top of the head. Leather long with plenty of feathering and wide enough so that when the dog is alert, the ears fan slightly forward to frame the face. **Skull** - Slightly rounded, but without dome or peak; it should appear flat because of the high placement of the ears. Stop is moderate, neither filled nor deep. **Muzzle** - Full muzzle slightly tapered. Length from base of stop to tip of nose about 1½ inches. Face well filled below eyes. Any tendency towards snipiness undesirable. Nose pigment uniformly black without flesh marks and nostrils well developed. Lips well developed but not pendulous giving a clean finish. Faults - Sharp or pointed muzzles. **Bite** - A perfect, regular and complete scissors bite is preferred, i.e. the upper teeth closely overlapping the lower teeth and set square into the jaws. Faults - undershot bite, weak or crooked teeth, crooked jaws.

Neck, Topline, Body: Neck - Fairly long, without throatiness, well enough muscled to form a slight arch at the crest. Set smoothly into nicely sloping shoulders to give an elegant look. **Topline** - Level both when moving and standing. **Body** - Short-coupled with ribs well sprung but not barrelled. Chest moderately deep, extending to elbows allowing ample heart room. Slightly less body at the flank than at the last rib, but with no tucked-up appearance. **Tail** - Well set on, carried happily but never much above the level of the back, and in constant characteristic motion when the dog is in action. Docking is optional. If docked, no more than one third to be removed.

Forequarters: Shoulders well laid back. Forelegs straight and well under the dog with elbows close to the sides. Pasterns strong and feet compact with well-cushioned pads. Dewclaws may be removed.

Hindquarters: The hindquarters construction should come down from a good broad pelvis, moderately muscled; stifles well turned and hocks well let down. The hindlegs when viewed from the rear should parallel each other from hock to heel. Faults - Cow or sickle hocks.

Coat: Of moderate length, silky, free from curl. Slight wave permissible. Feathering on ears, chest, legs and tail should be long, and the feathering on the feet is a feature of the breed. No trimming of the dog is permitted. Specimens where the coat has been altered by trimming, clipping, or by artificial means shall be so severely penalized as to be effectively eliminated from competition. Hair growing between the pads on the underside of the feet may be trimmed.

Color: Blenheim - Rich chestnut markings well broken up on a clear, pearly white ground. The ears must be chestnut and the color evenly spaced on the head and surrounding both eyes, with a white blaze between the eyes and ears, in the center of which may be the lozenge or "Blenheim spot." The lozenge is a unique and desirable, though not essential, characteristic of the Blenheim. **Tricolor** - Jet black markings well broken up on a clear, pearly white ground. The ears must be black and the color evenly spaced on the head and surrounding both eyes, with a white blaze between the eyes. Rich tan markings over the eyes, on cheeks, inside ears and on underside of tail. **Ruby** - Whole-colored rich red. **Black and Tan** - Jet black with rich, bright tan markings over eyes, on cheeks, inside ears, on chest, legs, and on underside of tail. Faults - Heavy ticking on Blenheims or Tricolors, white marks on Rubies or Black and Tans.

Gait: Free moving and elegant in action, with good reach in front and sound, driving rear action. When viewed from the side, the movement exhibits a good length of stride, and viewed from front and rear it is straight and true, resulting from straight-boned fronts and properly made and muscled hindquarters.

Temperament: Gay, friendly, non-aggressive with no tendency towards nervousness or shyness. Bad temper, shyness, and meanness are not to be tolerated and are to be severely penalized as to effectively remove the specimen from competition.

Approved Date: January 10, 1995 - Effective: April 30, 1995

AKC Official Standard for the Poodle:

The Standard for the Poodle (Toy variety) is the same as for the Standard and Miniature varieties, except as regards heights.

General Appearance: Carriage and Condition - That of a very active, intelligent and elegant appearing dog, squarely built, well proportioned, moving soundly and carrying himself proudly. Properly clipped in the traditional fashion and carefully groomed, the Poodle has about him an air of distinction and dignity peculiar to himself.

Size, Proportion, Substance: Size - The Standard Poodle is over 15 inches at the highest point of the shoulders. Any Poodle which is 15 inches or less in height shall be disqualified from competition as a Standard Poodle.

The Miniature Poodle is 15 inches or under at the highest point of the shoulders, with a minimum height in excess of 10 inches. Any Poodle which is over 15 inches or is 10 inches or less at the highest point of the shoulders shall be disqualified from competition as a Miniature Poodle.

The Toy Poodle is 10 inches or under at the highest point of the shoulders. Any Poodle which is more than 10 inches at the highest point of the shoulders shall be disqualified from competition as a Toy Poodle.

As long as the Toy Poodle is definitely a Toy Poodle, and the Miniature Poodle a Miniature Poodle, both in balance and proportion for the Variety, diminutiveness shall be the deciding factor when all other points are equal.

Proportion - To insure the desirable squarely built appearance, the length of body measured from the breastbone to the point of the rump approximates the height from the highest point of the shoulders to the ground.

Substance - Bone and muscle of both forelegs and hindlegs are in proportion to size of dog.

Head and Expression: (a) Eyes - very dark, oval in shape and set far enough apart and positioned to create an alert intelligent expression. Major fault: eyes round, protruding, large or very light. (b) Ears - hanging close to the head, set at or slightly below eye level. The ear leather is long, wide and thickly feathered; however, the ear fringe should not be of excessive length. (c) Skull - moderately rounded, with a slight but definite stop. Cheekbones and muscles flat. Length from occiput to stop about the same as length of muzzle. (d) Muzzle - long, straight and fine, with slight chiseling under the eyes. Strong without lippiness. The chin definite enough to preclude snipiness. Major fault: lack of chin. Teeth - white, strong and with a scissors bite. Major fault: undershot, overshot, wry mouth.

Neck, Topline, Body: Neck well proportioned, strong and long enough to permit the head to be carried high and with dignity. Skin snug at throat. The neck rises from strong, smoothly muscled shoulders. Major fault: ewe neck. The topline is level, neither sloping nor roached, from the highest point of the shoulder blade to the base of the tail, with the exception of a slight hollow just behind the shoulder. Body - (a) Chest deep and moderately wide with well sprung ribs. (b) The loin is short, broad and muscular. (c) Tail straight, set on high and carried up, docked of sufficient length to insure a balanced outline. Major fault: set low, curled, or carried over the back.

Forequarters: Strong, smoothly muscled shoulders. The shoulder blade is well laid back and approximately the same length as the upper foreleg. Major fault - steep shoulder. Forelegs - Straight and parallel when viewed from the front. When viewed from the side the elbow is directly below the highest point of the shoulder. The pasterns are strong. Dewclaws may be removed. Feet - The feet are rather small, oval in shape with toes well arched and cushioned on thick firm pads. Nails short but not excessively shortened. The feet turn neither in nor out. Major fault - paper or splay foot.

Hindquarters: The angulation of the hindquarters balances that of the forequarters. Hindlegs straight and parallel when viewed from the rear. Muscular with width in the region of the stifles which are well bent; femur and tibia are about equal in length; hock to heel short and perpendicular to the ground. When standing, the rear toes are only slightly behind the point of the rump. Major fault - cow-hocks.

Coat: (a) Quality - (1) Curly: of naturally harsh texture, dense throughout. (2) Corded: hanging in tight even cords of varying length; longer on mane or body coat, head, and ears; shorter on puffs, bracelets, and pompons. (b) Clip - A Poodle under 12 months may be shown in the "Puppy" clip. In all regular classes, Poodles 12 months or over must be shown in the "English Saddle" or "Continental" clip. In the Stud Dog and Brood Bitch classes and in a non-competitive Parade of Champions, Poodles may be shown in the "Sporting" clip. A Poodle shown in any other type of clip shall be disqualified. (1) "Puppy" - A Poodle under a year old may be shown in the "Puppy" clip with the coat long. The face, throat, feet and base of the tail are shaved. The entire shaven foot is visible. There is a pompon on the end of the tail. In order to give a neat appearance and a smooth unbroken line, shaping of the coat is permissible. (2) "English Saddle" - In the "English Saddle" clip, the face, throat, feet, forelegs and base of the tail are shaved, leaving puffs on the forelegs and a pompon on the end of the tail. The hindquarters are covered with a short blanket of hair except for a curved shaved area on each flank and two shaved bands on each hindleg. The entire shaven foot and a portion of the shaven leg above the puff are visible. The rest of the body is left in full coat but may be shaped in order to insure overall balance. (3) "Continental" - In the "Continental" clip, the face, throat, feet, and base of the tail are shaved. The hindquarters are shaved with pompons (optional) on the hips. The legs are shaved, leaving bracelets on the hindlegs and puffs on the forelegs. There is a pompon on the end of the tail. The entire shaven foot and a portion of the shaven foreleg above the puff are visible. The rest of the body is left in full coat but may be shaped in order to insure overall balance. (4) "Sporting" - In the "Sporting" clip, a Poodle shall be shown with face, feet, throat, and base of tail shaved, leaving a scissored cap on the top of the head and a pompon on the end of the tail. The rest of the body, and legs are clipped or scissored to follow the outline of the dog leaving a short blanket of coat no longer than one inch in length. The hair on the legs may be slightly longer than that on the body. In all clips the hair of the topknot may be left free or held in place by elastic bands. The hair is only of sufficient length to present a smooth outline. "Topknot" refers only to hair on the skull, from stop to occiput. This is the only area where elastic bands may be used.

Color: The coat is an even and solid color at the skin. In blues, grays, silvers, browns, cafe-aulaits, apricots and creams the coat may show varying shades of the same color. This is frequently present in the somewhat darker feathering of the ears and in the tipping of the ruff. While clear colors are definitely preferred, such natural variation in the shading of the coat is not to be considered a fault. Brown and cafe-au-lait Poodles have liver-colored noses, eye-rims and lips, dark toenails and dark amber eyes. Black, blue, gray, silver, cream and white Poodles have black noses, eye-rims and lips, black or self colored toenails and very dark eyes. In the apricots while the foregoing coloring is preferred, liver-colored noses, eye-rims and lips, and amber eyes are permitted but are not desirable. Major fault: color of nose, lips and eye-rims incomplete, or of wrong color for color of dog. Parti-colored dogs shall be disqualified. The coat of a parti-colored dog is not an even solid color at the skin but is of two or more colors.

Gait: A straightforward trot with light springy action and strong hindquarters drive. Head and tail carried up. Sound effortless movement is essential.

Temperament: Carrying himself proudly, very active, intelligent, the Poodle has about him an air of distinction and dignity peculiar to himself. Major fault: shyness or sharpness.

Major Faults: Any distinct deviation from the desired characteristics described in the Breed Standard.

Disqualifications: Size - A dog over or under the height limits specified shall be disqualified.
Clip - A dog in any type of clip other than those listed under coat shall be disqualified.
Particolors - The coat of a parti-colored dog is not an even solid color at the skin but of two or more colors. Parti-colored dogs shall be disqualified.

Value of Points

General appearance, temperament, carriage and condition.......30
Head, expression, ears, eyes and teeth.......20
Body, neck, legs, feet and tail.......20
Gait.......20
Coat, color and texture.......10

Approved August 14, 1984 - Reformatted March 27, 1990

Photo Credit: Eva Chamberlin of Cee Cee's Puppy Palace

Chapter 3 – Getting Serious About Adoption

If you have progressed past the stage of just considering a Cavapoo and are ready to adopt, we need to cover a few fundamentals. It's important that you go into a potential transaction armed with some basic information.

Photo Credit: Kirstin Pollington of Milky Paws

Is A Cavapoo Right for You?

Many dog owners make breed selections based on appearance alone and wind up regretting their choice. With the Cavapoo, people fall in love without thoroughly investigating the pros and cons of the breed.

It's a good idea, if possible, to spend some time with a Cavapoo before making your final decision. Clearly you will be meeting with breeders to discuss your potential adoption, but also consider contacting your local or regional kennel club to talk to Cavapoo owners. (You can also attend a dog show in your area.)

You are looking for people who will give you their honest opinion about the breed. Never adopt any dog until you've learned as much as possible about what it's really like to live with the breed.

We asked owner Dawn Smith if she made the right choice of breed: "We've had our Cavapoo Dughie-Doo for 4 years now and it is the best decision we have ever made. Dughie-Doo is the most sensible, responsible sensitive soul I have ever met. He is truly my heart dog. He understands every word I say to him, he keeps secrets and loves doing little jobs that just involve him."

Do You Need a License?

Before bringing your Cavapoo home, you need to think about whether there are any licensing restrictions in your area. Some countries have strict licensing requirements for the keeping of particular animals.

Even if you are not legally required to have a license for your Cavapoo, you might still want to consider getting one. Having a license for your dog means that there is an official record of your ownership, so should someone find your dog when he gets lost, that person will be able to find your contact information and reconnect you with him.

There are no federal regulations in the United States regarding the licensing of dogs, but most states do require that dogs be licensed by their owners; otherwise, you may be subject to a fine. Fortunately, dog licenses are inexpensive and fairly easy to obtain. Simply file an application with the state and renew the license each year. In most cases, licensing a dog costs no more than $25.

Selecting a Puppy

Everyone has their own strategy for selecting a puppy, and the breeder will certainly weigh in on this decision as well. I suggest that you go with the puppy that seems most drawn to you. I generally sit somewhat apart from the litter and wait for one of the dogs to come to me. For each puppy you "meet," consider the following basic evaluation.

Basic Evaluation Tips

As you are interacting with a puppy up for adoption, take the time to conduct the following evaluation, as these steps will help you to pick a healthy dog to take home:

- Puppies are often sleepy when you first meet them but then awaken quickly and become alert, energetic and even mischievous.

- The dog should feel well-nourished to the touch, with a little fat over the ribs. The overall appearance should be plump, healthy and rounded.

- Although the Cavapoo coat is short and rough, it should still appear healthy with no dandruff, bald patches or greasiness.

- Observe the puppy as it walks and runs. It's normal for little dogs to be wobbly, but there should be no sign of physical impairment like a limp or an odd gait.

- Healthy dogs have clear, bright eyes with no evident discharge in the corners or on the muzzle.

- Hold the puppy close to you and listen to its breathing. The sound should be quiet and steady with no coughing or sneezing. Check the nostrils to make sure they are free of any sign of discharge.

- Examine the area around the puppy's anus and genitals. Ensure there is no encrusted fecal matter or any sign of infection or pus.

- Test the dog's hearing by waiting until it is looking away from you and clap your hands. The dog should visibly react to the sound.

- To test visual acuity, roll a ball toward the puppy. The dog should notice the motion and react with accuracy in intercepting or investigating the toy.

Once you feel you can choose a puppy with some degree of confidence, start to work on a short list of breeders. Like most things in the modern world, you will likely turn to the Internet and visit breeder websites. I think you should first of all, try to find breeders within driving distance of your home (if possible), as you can then visit the facilities prior to actually taking one of the dogs.

Locating Cavapoo Breeders

We have approached the top Cavapoo breeders to enlist their help with this book. The contributors are listed near the front in the acknowledgements section.

You might also contact your local dog club or discuss your planned adoption with your vet. Advertisements in local or regional newspapers and magazines are an "iffy" matter at best. Often the dogs listed there are either the product of puppy mills or have been born to "backyard breeders."

Most backyard breeders are perfectly legitimate and well-intentioned people who have simply allowed their pets to breed. It isn't inherently a "bad" situation, but you will receive little if any verifiable information about the dogs.

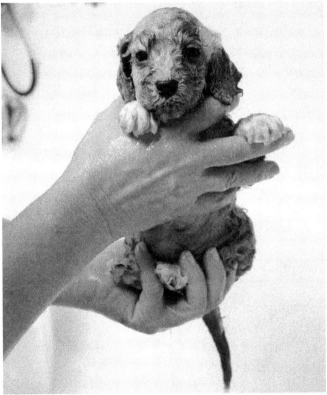

Photo Credit: Laura Koch of Petit Jean Puppies

Puppy mills, however, are much more disturbing and exist purely to make a profit. The dogs are generally kept in deplorable conditions with little if any health care and no socialization.

You should always be able to see where a puppy was born and evaluate the conditions in which it has been living. If you are not allowed to do so, be suspicious.

Even when you are dealing with breeders online (a ripe ground for puppy mills), modern technology should allow you to videoconference with the breeder, see the entire litter and the parents, and tour the facility.

This kind of "eyes on" evaluation, coupled with discussions with a knowledgeable breeder, are the foundation for a successful adoption. Responsible owners are so enthusiastic about the Cavapoo you can hardly stop them from talking about their dogs!

Always listen to your gut in dealing with people offering puppies for adoption. If you think something is "off" about the person and the facility, it probably is. Move on! And if you are sufficiently concerned that the dogs are being mistreated or exploited in any way, file a report with animal welfare.

Timing Your Adoption

Timing is more important in adopting a purebred dog than you might think. It is never a good sign when a facility tells you puppies are available year round. That's a definite red flag that you may be talking to a puppy mill.

The normal course of events is that you make contact with the breeder and your name is put on a waiting list. You may even be asked to place a small deposit to reserve a dog from a future litter. Generally if you decide not to adopt, the amount is refunded. Don't just assume this is the case, however. Always ask for details of any transaction.

Breeders are so protective about the health of their females that litters are only born once per year, usually in the spring and summer. Scheduling births for the warmer months allows more time to work with the dogs outdoors, which increases opportunities for socialization in a variety of settings.

You should also think about timing in regard to your own life. If you are involved in a major project at work or it's the holidays, bringing a puppy into the chaos may not be the best idea. Dogs are creatures of habit. They need routine to help them start a new life and learn to be reliable companions.

Pros and Cons of Owning a Cavapoo

Discussing the pros and cons of a breed draws me up short. I don't see the question as one that can be answered definitively. What one person loves about a breed might well drive another to the brink of insanity. Take the Jack Russell, for instance. It's a fantastically smart breed with the will of a Marine drill sergeant. This breed transcends the idea of alpha. I think they're great dogs, but I don't want to live with one!

A breeder should always be willing to discuss the positive and negatives of the Cavapoo and should help you decide if the breed is a good fit in your life. The one overriding concern should always be the welfare of the dogs. Cavapoo are exceptional dogs, and they deserve exceptional homes.

If you aren't sure whether a Cavapoo is the right choice, here's a brief summary of the pros and cons of this hybrid.

Advantages of Choosing a Cavapoo

• Cavapoos are loving, affectionate dogs that are perfect for family life. Although there can be exceptions they are usually not shy or timid, which makes them suitable for loud households.

• Cavapoos have one of the gentlest temperaments of any dog. They are almost never aggressive – as long as they have been properly socialized.

• Most Cavapoos become strongly attached to their owner. This makes them excellent companions.

• Both Cavaliers and Poodles are highly intelligent dogs. This makes Cavapoos a fun dog to train as they pick up new tricks and commands quickly.

• Cavapoos are also agile enough to take part in agility competitions.

• The small size of the Cavapoo makes them perfect for apartments. They usually need one proper walk per day.

• Some Cavapoos inherit the non-shedding gene from the Poodle. Cavaliers usually shed more than Poodles, so the amount of shedding depends on which genes are dominant.

• Cavapoos love spending time with people. They are always at their happiest when with their owners. Cavapoos also love hugs and will happily sleep in front of the TV or fire.

Disadvantages of Choosing a Cavapoo

• When buying a crossbreed, you can never be sure which traits, characteristics and hereditary conditions are passed on from parents. You can minimize the risks by making sure you meet the parent dogs and asking whether they have been tested for genetic conditions.

• Cavapoos are known to be excitable dogs. This can develop into hyperactivity in some cases, especially if the dog is part of a high-energy household. Providing lots of exercise and mental stimulation can reduce the chance of hyper behavior.

• The Cavapoo is friendly to almost all strangers. This is a good thing if you have lots of visitors but means the hybrid isn't suitable for guard dog duties.

• While the Cavapoo doesn't require extensive grooming, you should be prepared to brush the coat often to avoid matting. Cavapoos that have inherited the Poodle's coat usually need to be brushed more regularly to prevent matting.

• Most owners take their Cavapoos to the groomers and get their coats clipped as a result of low to non-shedding coats, therefore this is a cost to bear in mind in advance.

• The Cavapoo is a highly social dog. This means that it shouldn't be left alone for long periods. If you work during the day, a Cavapoo may not be the right choice.

• Cavapoos are easy to train, but they often have a stubborn streak! This means Cavapoos will pick up a command quickly but need plenty of additional training to make sure they follow it at all times. This is common with intelligent dogs, and fortunately a Cavapoo's desire to please often overcomes its stubbornness.

How Much Do Cavapoos Cost?

Cavapoos are relatively expensive dogs and can cost more than many purebreds. The price of a Cavapoo puppy depends on factors such as the health of the parents, gender, color and breeder. The price also varies by country – Cavapoo puppies are particularly expensive in the UK.

• United Kingdom: Cavapoo puppies in the UK typically cost around £600-£800, although the most expensive can be sold for £1000 or more.

• Australia: The average price for a Cavapoo in Australia is approximately AU$300-AU$500. Some of the top breeders, however, sell their Cavapoos for as much as AU$1800.

• United States: The price of Cavapoos in the US varies depending on location. The average price is approximately $1000-$2500. Some breeders charge considerably more than this, especially those that have a waiting list for puppies.

These websites can be good places to begin your search:

Adopt a Pet — http://www.adoptapet.com
Petango — http://www.petango.com
Puppy Find — http://www.puppyfind.com/
Oodle - http://dogs.oodle.com/

Dena Fidanza of Dena's Doggies in the USA says: "There are very few breeders in the US at this time (I get calls from all over the country). Some are asking under $1000, but I have been told by customers that they did not want to get out of the car at the location or asked to meet at another location other than where the puppies had been raised - which is a BIG warning sign."

Consider borrowing a dog for a couple of days whilst the owner is on holiday to get a good feel of the type of breed you are looking for. There are now websites offering these services i.e. https://www.borrowmydoggy.com/

Chapter 4 – Buying a Cavapoo

When you first meet a litter of adorable Cavapoo puppies, it's easy to forget that many problems occur later in life. It's usually not possible to identify a dog's health problems or bad behaviors at a young age. This means it's vital to ask the right questions of the breeder.

Photo Credit: Jackie Arana of My Cavapoos

The process of buying a Cavapoo is similar to buying any other breed; however, there are some extra considerations when looking for a Cavapoo:

• Choose a breeder who has completed genetic health testing on both the Poodle and Cavalier. This doesn't guarantee that the puppy won't develop a health problem but reduces the chances.

• You should ask about the history of both the grandparents and great grandparents. Genetic conditions can skip generations, so it's useful to know the health of the puppy's ancestors. Mitral Valve Disease and Syringomyelia are two diseases you should always discuss with a Cavapoo breeder.

• For a greater chance of adopting a dog without health conditions, consider adopting an adult Cavapoo. Many of the conditions associated with Cavapoos are not obvious as a puppy. When buying a healthy adult dog, there is a reduced chance of undiscovered serious health conditions.

• Ask to meet both the Cavalier and Poodle. This isn't always possible but can be a big help when trying to judge the future character of the puppy.

• Also ask whether the breeder has a policy if the puppy develops a genetic condition. Many of the best breeders have a refund policy for genetic conditions that only become apparent later in life.

Aside from Cavapoo-specific questions, there are best practices that apply when choosing any dog. These include:

• Before you visit the puppy, call the seller and find out more about the litter. You should ask whether the seller bred the puppies, where the puppies are kept, have they had any vaccinations and how many puppies were born in the same litter.

• If a breeder refuses to answer your questions or you feel that they are being evasive, end the conversation and try a different seller. Breeders should always be willing to discuss the dogs they are selling.

• When you visit, make sure you see the puppy with its mother. The behavior of the mother is likely to be similar to the puppy's eventual personality.

• Ask whether the breeder continues to provide support and advice after you bring your puppy home. The best breeders are happy to help you integrate the puppy into your life.

• Talk to the breeder about the health conditions associated with both breeds. A breeder should have a strong understanding of potential genetic problems affecting his or her dogs.

• It's a good idea to ask for a written contract that contains the responsibilities of both you and the breeder.

Nowadays many breeders are home based and their dogs live in the house as pets. Puppies are typically raised in the breeder's home, as well. It's very common for Cavapoo breeders to use guardian homes for their breeding dogs. A guardian home is a permanent family for the dog. The breeder retains ownership of the dog during the years the dog is used for breeding; however, the dog lives with the guardian family.

This arrangement is great for the dog because once retired from breeding, they are spayed/neutered and returned to their forever family. There is no need to re-home the dog after its breeding career has ended. There are still breeders who use kennels, but the numbers of home breeders are quite high.

While I advocate buying locally, with the Cavapoo this is not always possible. Windie Sturges of Calla Lily Cavapoo explains: "I personally offer "Nanny Transport" where the puppies fly on board the plane with me. I also have not only our website, but also videos so people can see "all of us" when they are too far to come to us. We work hard to transition our puppies to their new homes with the least amount of stress."

Questions You Must Answer

Breeders want to know their dogs are going to good homes. You will be asked questions about such things as your home, work schedule, family and other pets. This should not be considered prying but an excellent sign that you are working with a professional with a genuine interest in placing their dogs appropriately.

You want the breeder to be a resource for you in the future if you need help or guidance in living with your Cavapoo. Be receptive to answering your breeder's queries and open to having an ongoing friendship.

It is quite common for breeders to call and check on how their dogs are doing and to make themselves available to answer questions.

What the Breeder Should Provide to You

All of the following items should be provided to you as part of the adoption process, and you should receive complete answers to all questions you have regarding any of these provisions or others included in the transaction:

- **Contract of sale.** This document should detail the responsibilities of both parties and explain the transfer of the registration papers.

- **Information packet.** This material should include advice on feeding, training and exercise as well as health procedures like worming and vaccinations.

- **All health records.** You should be given copies of all health records for the puppy (and parents); in particular, the schedule of vaccinations and required boosters. Full disclosure of any potential genetic conditions associated with the breed should accompany these records, as well as the results of any testing or screening performed. Note that while screening or testing obviously helps reduce risks, there can never be a complete guarantee that future problems will not occur.

- **Health guarantee.** The guarantee confirms the health of the puppy at the time of the adoption with a stipulation that this fact be confirmed with a vet within a specified time period. There should also be a detailed explanation of recompense in the event that a health condition does arise within the length of the guarantee.

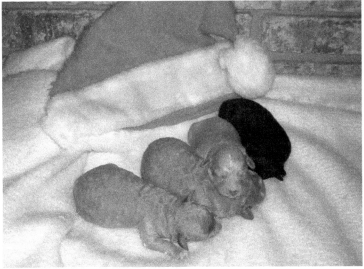

Photo Credit: Dena Fidanza of Dena's Doggies

Warning Signs of a Bad Breeder

Each of the following scenarios indicate you may be working with a bad breeder. Do not gloss over any of these red flags:

- Being told there is no need for you to come to the breeder's home or kennel in person.

- Assurances that buying a puppy sight unseen is normal.

- Refusal to allow clients to see where the dogs are currently living.

- Overcrowded conditions in which the dogs are apprehensive and nervous around people.

- No access to meet either of the puppy's parents and no access to verifiable information about them.

- No medical records for the dogs or promises the records will be sent "later."

- Failure to provide a health guarantee.

- No signed bill of sale or promises that one will be forwarded.

Beware of "breeders" who tell you they have rare colors with names not noted in the standard. These color breeders are usually backyard breeders in it to sell "rare color dogs" for extortionate amounts.

Avoiding Scam Puppy Sales

Cavapoos are one of the cutest crossbreeds. This has unfortunately led to them becoming a popular choice for puppy mills. These puppies are often sold in pet shops and are labeled as being bred by an "ethical breeder." This simply isn't true -

ethical breeders always want to be sure that trustworthy families adopt their dogs.

When buying from a puppy mill it is almost impossible to judge the health of the dog. Puppy farms also don't care about the long-term health of their dogs – they just want to breed as many as possible.

Aside from health conditions, puppies bred by mills are often removed from their litter much too early. This leads to behavioral problems such as aggression, shyness or biting. In short, you should always avoid buying a Cavapoo from a pet shop or puppy farm.

Look out as well for scammers who will advertise a single puppy on the free-to-advertise websites and get you to pay a "deposit" over the Internet. They leave the advert open long enough to rake in a number of deposits then remove the ad and create a new one from a different location.

Unfortunately, the Internet is full of these kinds of operations, as are many pet stores. If you don't have the money to work with a breeder, think about a shelter or rescue adoption. Even if you can't be certain of adopting a Cavapoo, you CAN be certain you will be helping an animal in need.

Best Age to Purchase a Cavapoo Puppy

A Cavapoo puppy needs time to learn important life skills from the mother dog, including eating solid food and grooming themselves.

For the first month of a puppy's life, he will be on a mother's milk-only diet. Once the puppy's teeth begin to appear, he will start to be weaned from mother's milk, and by the age of 8 weeks should be completely weaned and eating just puppy food.

Puppies generally leave between 8-9 weeks and are usually weaned before they receive their first vaccines. It is not beneficial for the pup to stay longer, as it can have a negative affect for several reasons. One is that the puppy should not have access to nursing after his first vaccine, otherwise that vaccine is void. Some moms will continue to nurse despite the puppy being on solid food.

In other cases, the mom is too overwhelmed with the size of the pups and the size of the litter and she avoids them. This occurs as early as 6 weeks old and can result in bad behaviors as the puppies interact with each other. Their roughhouse playing becomes more and more imprinted on them, and families could struggle to teach the puppy not to play with children as they do with their litter mates.

Trainers would even highly recommend training and bonding begin with their new families by 8-10 weeks. In addition, pups need to be highly socialized between 8-12 weeks with new people, new experiences and places. This time period is very crucial in developing a well-rounded pup.

How to Choose a Puppy?

My best advice is to go with the puppy that is drawn to you. My standard strategy in selecting a pup has always been to sit a little apart from a litter and let one of the dogs come to me. My late father was, in his own way, a "dog whisperer." He taught me this trick for picking puppies, and it's never let me down.

I've had dogs in my life since childhood and enjoyed a special connection with them all. Often the dog that comes to me isn't the one I might have chosen, but I still rely on this method.

You will want to choose a puppy with a friendly, easy-going temperament, and your breeder should be able to help you with your selection. Also ask the breeder about the temperament and personalities of the puppy's parents and if they have socialized the puppies.

Always be certain to ask if a Cavapoo puppy you are interested in has displayed any signs of aggression or fear, because if this is happening at such an early age, you may experience behavioral troubles as the puppy becomes older.

Photo Credit: Honey by Charlotte G Photography

Beyond this, I suggest that you interact with your dog with a clear understanding that each one is an individual with unique traits. It is not so much a matter of learning about all Cavapoos, but rather of learning about YOUR Cavapoo.

Checking Puppy Social Skills

When choosing a puppy out of a litter, look for one that is friendly and outgoing, rather than one who is overly aggressive or fearful.

Puppies who demonstrate good social skills with their litter mates are much more likely to develop into easy-going, happy adult dogs that play well with others.

Observe all the puppies together and take notice:

Which puppies are comfortable both on top and on the bottom when play fighting and wrestling with their litter mates and which puppies seem to only like being on top?

Which puppies try to keep the toys away from the other puppies and which puppies share?

Which puppies seem to like the company of their litter mates and which ones seem to be loners?

Puppies that ease up or stop rough play when another puppy yelps or cries are more likely to respond appropriately when they play too roughly as adults.

Is the puppy sociable with humans? If he will not come to you or display fear toward strangers, this could develop into a problem later in their life.

Is the puppy relaxed about being handled? If he is not, he may become difficult with adults and children during daily interactions, grooming or visits to the veterinarian's office.

Chapter 5 – Bringing Your Cavapoo Home

Good preparation in advance will help, as well as a complete understanding of the fact that all puppies are work!

This is an important stage in your Cavapoo's life and one that demands your active attention and involvement. A dog's adult behavior and temperament are shaped during those first weeks in a new home. It's your responsibility to ensure the dog receives the necessary support and training to be a well-mannered, obedient companion.

Photo Credit: Paul & Michele Flower owner of Wally

Some of the specific tasks you want to accomplish early in your relationship include the following:

- Puppy proofing the house before your pet arrives
- Buying the equipment for crate and house training
- Deciding how you will manage a healthy diet
- Learning the grooming protocol appropriate for the breed
- Planning a program of socialization

In these opening weeks, you will want to get ahead of negative behaviors like jumping, whining and barking. If you don't have the time to spend working with your dog in the areas that will make him a desirable companion, ask yourself if this is really the time in your life to have a pet. Cavapoos, as a breed, are not needy dogs; therefore, they should not suffer from separation anxiety as long as they are correctly trained.

Bear in mind that you are also your dog's companion. This is not a one-sided relationship. What is your work schedule? Do you have to travel often and for extended periods? Be responsible and only adopt one of these dogs if you have time to spend with your pet.

There is one undeniable truth about all puppies of all breeds. No matter his size, a puppy can get into big trouble fast. Cavapoo puppies are no exception. Before you even think about bringing your new dog home, you must "puppy proof" the house.

Puppy Proofing 101

It's best to think of your new puppy as a super intelligent, four-legged toddler. His mind is as bright and inventive as that of any child, but it comes with a set of teeth bent on destruction and mayhem. Every single thing in your home that can be sniffed, chewed, swallowed, or some combination thereof is free game and therefore in danger.

Household Poisons

Dogs will eat anything, especially when they're puppies. A young dog just gulps down whatever is in his path with no forethought, putting him at serious risk for accidental poisoning.

Thoroughly examine any area in the home to which the dog will have access or into which he could gain access. Take away any potential poisons, or get them high up and out of the dog's reach. The better option is really to take them out to the garage or to another outbuilding. You want to be particularly vigilant about:

- Cleaning products
- Insecticides
- Mothballs
- Fertilizers
- Antifreeze

When in doubt, get it out. Caution is always the best policy. If you don't know that an item is poisonous, assume that it is. Your puppy should not have access to any type of chemical whatsoever.

Look Around with the Eyes of a Puppy

Puppies investigate everything! Nothing escapes their attention. To really protect your new "baby," get down on the floor at his eye level. When you see things from his perspective, all kinds of hazards you never dreamed existed in your home become evident.

- Look for anything that dangles – drapery pulls, electrical cords, frayed threads on upholstery and loose wallpaper. Remove or contain those items in some way. Cord minders are a good solution.

- Locate "lost" items that have found their way under your furniture or have become wedged between the furniture cushions. All of these items can be choking hazards. The fact that they are "hidden" and have to be "dug up" will make them all the more enticing.

- Spot "topple" dangers. Puppies love to play tug of war. That's fine if you're on the other end of the rope, but if the "opponent" is the television tethered to a coaxial cable, the whole unit can easily come crashing down.

- Prepare for the chewing. Young dogs will gnaw on anything. Remove all the stuffed items, including sofa pillows, and wrap the legs of prized furniture to protect them.

Anything that could even remotely look like a toy should be taken out of the room. Think I'm exaggerating? Go to your favorite search engine online and type in "dog chewed cell phone." You won't believe what a determined puppy can do!

Plant Dangers, Inside and Out

Both indoor and outdoor plants present a risk, but the list is far longer than most people realize. There's a fair degree of awareness that peach and apricot pits are potentially poisonous, but so are spinach leaves and tomato vines.

The American Society for the Prevention of Cruelty to Animals has created a large reference list of plants for dog owners here.

http://www.aspca.org/pet-care/animal-poison-control/toxic-and-non-toxic-plants

Even the plants that are not potentially lethal can cause severe and painful gastrointestinal upset. It's a myth that dogs will leave house plants alone. When I say puppies will chew anything, I mean anything — including your plants.

Preparing for the Homecoming

In addition to a travel crate for the ride home, get a couple of puppy-safe chew toys. Put those items inside the crate with some piece of clothing you've worn recently. This will help your new pet to learn your scent and to begin to see you as the leader of his "pack." Don't forget to secure the crate in place with the seatbelt.

Ask the breeder to schedule a time for you to pick up your dog in between regular meals. You don't want the puppy getting sick on the ride home. Be sure to take the dog to do his "business" before he gets in the car and again as soon as you arrive home. Always praise a puppy for going in the right spot at the right time.

The ride home will include a lot of whining and crying, which you need to resist. If you don't, you're very smart new pet will immediately peg you for the pushover you are and begin training you to answer his every whim. Beyond any other considerations, a small dog is much safer in a crate in a moving vehicle than riding on someone's lap.

Ask a friend to go with you and ride in the back seat with the puppy (in the crate). Sometimes just a comforting presence is all it takes for a little dog to settle down and go right to sleep.

The transition from the breeder to your home should be low key. Don't overwhelm the puppy. If you have children, explain that the trip home needs to be quiet and calm since the puppy is leaving its mother and siblings for the first time. Ask your kids to stay at home and to be patient about allowing the little dog to settle into his new home when you do arrive.

Take the puppy to the area of the house that has been puppy proofed and let him explore. At the same time, you don't want to overload the dog's senses, you also don't want him to feel isolated and nervous. Resist the urge to pick him up every time he cries.

Follow the feeding schedule to which the dog has become accustomed at the breeders. Routines comfort dogs and give them a sense of safety. Often breeders will provide a small supply of whatever food the puppy is used to eating.

Continue to use articles of worn clothing to reassure and comfort the puppy and consider leaving a radio playing on low at night so the little dog doesn't feel so alone. A warm water bottle wrapped in soft cloth can also help.

If you bring the puppy to bed with you, be prepared to have your pet there for life. If you want a dog that will sleep through the night in its crate, ignore the pitiful whining.

The Importance of the Crate

A crate can make the first few months of owning a Cavapoo much easier. Crates can speed up potty training, provide a useful "time-out" zone and also give the dog a place to relax.

It's important to understand that a crate isn't a cage. It is a legitimate training tool that can make potty training a Cavapoo much easier. When properly introduced to a crate, most dogs learn to feel safe and secure inside.

Cavapoo puppies, like many breeds, can have excitable moments. This often happens when the puppy is overtired and doesn't know that it's time to calm down! Crates are great for giving your puppy permission to relax. You shouldn't leave your Cavapoo in the crate for too long – or use it as a punishment – but for the occasional "time-out," you'll be glad you have one!

It's important to buy the right size and type of crate. If a crate is too small your dog won't feel comfortable. A crate that's too big allows your puppy to treat half as his den and the other as a toilet. As a general rule, your dog should be able to turn around, stand up comfortably and lie down in the crate. Once potty trained, you can buy a larger crate for your dog.

There are a number of types of crate. The most common are:

• Wire crates. Wire crates are great for Cavapoos because they allow cooling airflow. The Cavapoo's thick coat can make it easy for them to overheat in a plastic or soft crate. Wire crates are also great for potty training, as you can use dividers to make the right sized internal area.

• Soft crates. Soft crates are the most portable but are also difficult to clean. This makes them unsuitable for potty training. For transporting a Cavapoo, soft crates can be a good option.

• Plastic crates. Plastic crates are less noisy than wire crates and can be bought in a variety of colors. It's also difficult for a dog to break out of a plastic crate. The downside is that plastic crates provide limited airflow, which is a problem for fluffy Cavapoos.

If you aren't sure which type of crate to buy for a new Cavapoo puppy, go with a wire crate. They are strong and cooler for the dog. You can also buy a full-size wire crate and use a divider for potty training, rather than buying a smaller crate and replacing it as your dog grows.

Slow Introductions with the Children

For the safety and comfort of all concerned, supervise your children's interactions with the new puppy. Children must be taught to handle all animals safely and with kindness.

Don't let the kids wear the puppy out during its first day or two at home. Let the dog have time to adjust.

Photo Credit: Charlotte Purkiss of Lotties Cavapoos

What Can I Do to Make My Cavapoo Love Me?

From the moment you bring your Cavapoo dog home, every minute you spend with him is an opportunity to bond. The earlier you start working with your dog, the more quickly that bond will grow and the closer you and your Cavapoo will become.

While simply spending time with your Cavapoo will encourage the growth of that bond, there are a few things you can do to purposefully build your bond with your dog. Some of these things include:

• Take your Cavapoo for daily walks during which you frequently stop to pet and talk to your dog.

• Engage your Cavapoo in games like fetch and hide-and-seek to encourage interaction.

• Interact with your dog through daily training sessions – teach your dog to pay attention when you say his name.

• Be calm and consistent when training your dog – always use positive reinforcement rather than punishment.

• Spend as much time with your Cavapoo as possible, even if it means simply keeping the dog in the room with you while you cook dinner or pay bills.

Common Mistakes to Avoid

Never pick your Cavapoo puppy up if they are showing fear or aggression toward an object, another dog or person, because this will be rewarding them for unbalanced behavior.

If they are doing something you do not want them to continue, your puppy needs to be gently corrected by you with firm and calm energy, so that they learn not to react with fear or aggression. When the mum of the litter tells her puppies off, she will use a deep noise with strong eye contact until the puppy quickly realizes it's doing something naughty.

Don't play the "hand" game where you slide the puppy across the floor with your hands just because it's amusing for humans to see a little ball of fur scrambling to collect themselves and run back across the floor for another go.

This sort of "game" will teach your puppy to disrespect you as his leader in two different ways — first, because this "game" teaches him that humans are his play toys, and secondly, this type of "game" teaches him that humans are a source of excitement.

When Cavapoo puppies are teething, they will naturally want to chew on everything within reach, and this will include you. As cute as you might think it is when they are young puppies, this is not an acceptable behavior, and you need to gently, but firmly, discourage the habit, just like a mother dog does to her puppies when they need to be weaned.

Always praise your puppy when he stops inappropriate behavior, as this is the beginning of teaching him to understand rules and boundaries. Often we humans are quick to discipline puppies or dogs for inappropriate behavior, but we forget to praise them for their good behavior.

Don't treat your Cavapoo like a small, furry human. When people try to turn dogs into humans, this can cause them much stress and confusion that could lead to behavioral problems.

Well-behaved Cavapoos thrive on rules and boundaries, and when they understand that there is no question you are their leader and they are your follower, they will live a contented, happy and stress-free life.

Dogs are a different species with different rules; for example, they do not naturally cuddle, and they need to learn to be stroked and cuddled by humans. Therefore, be careful when approaching a dog for the first time and being overly expressive with your hands. The safest areas to touch are the back and chest, avoid patting on the head and touching the ears.

Many people will assume that a dog that is yawning is tired when, in fact, it may be a signal of being uncomfortable or nervous.

Be careful when staring at dogs because this is one of the ways in which they threaten each other. This body language can make them feel distinctly uneasy.

Introductions with Other Pets

Cavapoos have a reputation for getting along moderately well with other animals in the family. The most tentative first meeting will likely be with the family cat.

Because I know Cavapoos that live in peace with other animals, I'm offering you the complete range of conventional wisdom in regard to this aspect of Cavapoo ownership. That being said, I would not personally keep a Cavapoo and a cat.

This is mainly because I am also a great lover of cats and could never live with myself if I created a situation where I placed a living creature in danger by bringing it into my home with a potentially aggressive dog.

The greatest trouble with introductions is more apt to occur when you are bringing animals into a home with an adult Cavapoo. You stand a greater chance of success introducing a puppy into a home with existing pets.

Older dogs have ways of putting puppies in their place, usually with a warning growl or bared teeth. This "instructional" behavior isn't something you typically need to worry about. If there are older dogs in the house, make sure they are still getting enough of your attention and allow the hierarchy of the pack to assert itself.

For cats already in residence, the tried and true method of arranging an introduction with a puppy is behind a closed bathroom door. This lets the cat sniff the dog and get used to its scent without having to deal with offensive, in-your-whiskers puppy exuberance. The primary problem cats have with dogs is they are just too effusive and have no respect for feline personal space.

When it comes time for the first face-to-face meeting, don't overreact. If you're upset and nervous, your pets will pick up on your feelings, and the added tension doesn't help the situation. If there is an altercation, don't yell. Just separate the animals and try again another day.

Truth be told, when a puppy meets a fully "weaponized" house cat, the chances are far greater that the little dog is the one that will be sent running away yelping. Again, so long as there's no real harm being inflicted on either party, be quiet, issue a firm "no" complete with disapproving glare, and let the animals sort it out for themselves.

While this might not work with all breeds, Cavapoos are highly intelligent and learn quickly. The cat may not ever love the dog, but an overall state of detente will be created over time. Cats have a tremendous capacity to ignore people, creatures, and things they do not like.

In a first meeting with another dog, it's generally a good idea to have two people in the room just in case the animals have to be quickly separated and removed to different areas. Your manner always sets the tone, so if you're calm, friendly, and happy, chances are the dogs will be as well.

Puppies most often run into trouble with their elders because they don't understand the etiquette adult dogs use not to overstep territorial bounds. Let the older dog teach those lessons, but do exercise caution at mealtimes. Perceived competition for food can lead to nasty aggressive spats. It's best that all dogs (and cats) have their own bowls and preferably their own place to eat in peace.

Habituation and Socialization

Habituation is when you continuously provide exposure to the same stimuli over a period of time. This will help your Cavapoo to relax in his environment and will teach him how to behave around unfamiliar people, noises, other pets and different surroundings. Expose your Cavapoo puppy continuously to new sounds and new environments.

When you allow for your Cavapoo to face life's positive experiences through socialization and habituation, you're helping your Cavapoo to build a library of valuable information that he can use when he's faced with a difficult situation. If he's had plenty of wonderful and positive early experiences, the more likely he'll be able to bounce back from any surprising or scary situations.

When your Cavapoo puppy arrives at his new home for the first time, he'll start bonding with his human family immediately. This will be his primary bond. His secondary bond will be with everyone outside your home. A dog should never be secluded inside his home. Be sure to find the right balance where you're not exposing your Cavapoo puppy to too much external stimuli. If he starts becoming fearful, speak to your veterinarian.

The puppyhood journey can be tiresome yet very rewarding. Primary socialization starts between three and five weeks of age where a pup's experiences take place within his litter. This will have a huge impact on all his future emotional behavior.

Photo Credit: Louise Driscoll - owner of Walter

Socialization from six to twelve weeks allows for puppies to bond with other species outside of their litter mates and parents. It's at this particular stage that most pet parents will bring home a puppy and where he'll soon become comfortable with humans, other pets and children.

By the time a puppy is around twelve to fourteen weeks, he becomes more difficult to introduce to new environments and new people and starts showing suspicion and distress.

Nonetheless, if you've recently adopted a Cavapoo puppy or are bringing one home and he's beyond this ideal age, don't neglect to continue the socialization process. Puppies need to be exposed to as many new situations, environments, people and other animals as possible, and it is never too late to start.

During puppyhood, you can easily teach your puppy to politely greet a new person, yet by the time a puppy has reached social maturity, the same puppy, if not properly socialized, may start lunging forward and acting aggressively, with the final outcome of lunging and nipping.

Never accidentally reward your Cavapoo puppy for displaying fear or growling at another dog or animal by picking him up. Picking up your Cavapoo at this time, actually turns out to be a reward for him, and you will be teaching him to continue with this type of behavior. As well, picking up a puppy literally places him in a "top dog" position where he is higher and more dominant.

The correct action to take in such a situation is to gently correct your puppy with a firm yet calm energy by distracting him with a "No," so that he learns to let you deal with the situation on his behalf.

If you allow fearful or nervous puppies to deal with situations that unnerve them all by themselves, they may learn to react with fear or aggression, and you will have created a problem that could escalate into something quite serious as they grow older.

The same is true of situations where young puppies may feel the need to protect themselves from a bigger or older dog that may come charging in for a sniff. It is the guardian's responsibility to protect the puppy so that he does not think he must react with fear or aggression in order to protect himself.

Once your Cavapoo puppy has received all his vaccinations, you can take him out to public dog parks and various locations where many dogs are found.

Before allowing your puppy to interact with other dogs or puppies, take him for a disciplined walk on leash so that he will be a little tired and less likely to immediately engage with all other dogs.

You will want to keep your puppy on leash and close beside you because most puppies are a bundle of out-of-control energy. They need you to protect and teach them how far they can go before getting themselves into trouble with adult dogs who may not appreciate excited puppy playfulness.

If your puppy shows any signs of aggression or dominance toward another dog, you must immediately step in and calmly discipline him.

Take your puppy everywhere with you and introduce him to many different people of all ages, sizes and ethnicities. Most people will come to you and want to interact with your puppy. If they ask if they can hold your puppy, let them, because so long as they are gentle and don't drop the puppy, this is a good way to socialize your Cavapoo and show him that humans are friendly.

As important as socialization is, it is also important that the dog be left alone for short periods when young so that he can cope with some periods of isolation. If an owner goes out and the puppy has never experienced this, he may destroy things or make a mess because of panic. Your puppy is thinking he is vulnerable and could be attacked by something or someone coming into the house.

Dogs that have been socialized are able to easily diffuse a potentially troublesome situation and avoid fights. Dogs that are poorly socialized often misinterpret or do not understand the subtle signals of other dogs, getting into trouble as a result.

Photo Credit: Dena Fidanza of Dena's Doggies

Creating a Safe Environment

Never think for a minute that your Cavapoo would not bolt and run away. Even well-adjusted, happy puppies and adult dogs can run away, usually in extreme conditions such as with fireworks, thunder or when scared.

Collar, tag and microchip your new Cavapoo. Microchipping is not enough, since many pet parents tend to presume that dogs without collars are homeless or have been abandoned.

Recent photos of your Cavapoo with the latest clip need to be placed in your wallet or purse.

Train your Cavapoo – foster and work with a professional, positive trainer to ensure that your Cavapoo does not run out the front door or out the backyard gate. Teach your Cavapoo basic, simple commands such as "come" and "stay."

Create a special, fun digging area just for him, hide his bones and toys and let your Cavapoo know that it's okay to dig in that area. After all, dogs need to play!

Introduce your new, furry companion to all your neighbors so everyone will know that he belongs to you.

Puppy Nutrition

The most successful nutritional programs for dogs are those that track your pet's growth. Puppies aged four months and under need four meals per day. That can be reduced to three feedings in months 4-8, and then two feedings for life-- morning and evening.

Your puppy's feeding schedule is an addendum to his housebreaking. Don't "free feed" a young dog, which is the practice of having dry food out at all times. This may work for an adult if weight gain is not an issue, but regular feeding times for a puppy set the pattern for trips outside.

Put the food down and leave it for 10-20 minutes, then take it up — even if your dog hasn't "finished." You are not depriving your pet but instead getting him accustomed to a routine that will help you both.

Rely on premium, high quality dry food. Your best option is to give your Cavapoo whatever he's been eating at the breeder. If you want to transition your pet to a different product, the change should only occur slowly and over time. Sudden dietary changes throw puppies into major gastrointestinal upset.

To make an effective food transition, mix the existing diet with the new food, slowly changing the percentage of new to old over a period of 10 days.

The vast majority of breeders recommend not feeding puppy food. It can be high in protein and actually can cause the puppy to grow too fast, thus possibly creating bone growth issues.

Always read the label on any food you are using. The first ingredients listed should be meat or fishmeal. High percentages of meat by-products and cornmeal indicate a food with low nutritional value. It will fill your pet up and increase his production of waste but do little to provide the required vitamins and minerals.

Grain free is often recommended for the Cavapoo. Many are allergic to corn, wheat and some other grains. Also no "soy" in the dog food – it irritates them!

Puppies should not receive wet food. It is too rich for their digestion, lacks the correct nutritional balance, and is harder to measure. Portion control is crucial with young dogs. A puppy should only receive the amount of food that is right for his age and weight, information that should be provided on the label of the dog food sack.

To avoid messy "tip overs," use weighted stainless steel food and water bowls. Plastic retains odors and breeds bacteria. Bowls in elevated stands create a better posture for the dog while eating, just make sure the arrangement is not too tall for the puppy to reach.

Stainless steel bowl sets sell for less than $25 / £14.87. (Those with an included stand may be priced slightly higher.)

Adult Nutrition

The same basic principles should guide your management of an adult Cavapoo diet. Pick a product line that offers a graduated program of nutrition from a puppy formula, through an adult mix, and finally a senior blend. This creates the perfect arrangement for consistent nutrition for life with seamless transitions from one food to the next.

No Table Scraps!

All dogs are accomplished beggars. Don't let this unhealthy dietary habit get started! Even when you give your dog proper canine treats, those items should never constitute more than 5% of the total daily food intake. This caution is not just in reference to weight gain. Many human foods are toxic to dogs, including, but not limited to:

- Chocolate
- Raisins
- Alcohol
- Human vitamins (especially those with iron)
- Mushrooms

- Onions and garlic
- Walnuts
- Macadamia nuts
- Raw fish
- Raw pork
- Raw chicken

Any bones given to a puppy should be too large to swallow. Bones are both a choke and "splinter" hazard. The sharp pieces can lacerate the throat and intestines. Supervise a dog chewing on a bone and take the item away at the first sign of splintering.

There is an idea that a dog "should" be given animal bones. I am against this practice. There are excellent "puppy safe" chew products that are also beneficial to keep your pet's teeth clean and in good shape. These commercial products are a much better and safer option.

The Canine Teeth and Jaw

Even today, there are too many dog food choices that have far more to do with being convenient for us humans to serve than they do with being a well-balanced, healthy food choice for a canine.

In order to choose the right food for your Cavapoo, first it's important to understand a little bit about canine physiology and what Mother Nature intended when she created our furry companions.

While humans are omnivores who can derive energy from eating plants, our canine companions are carnivores, which means they derive their energy and nutrient requirements from eating a diet consisting mainly or exclusively of the flesh of animals, birds or fish.

Unlike humans, who are equipped with wide, flat molars for grinding grains, vegetables and other plant-based materials, canine teeth are all pointed because they are designed to rip, shred and tear into meat and bone.

Photo Credit: Charlotte Purkiss of Lotties Cavapoos

Another obvious consideration when choosing an appropriate food source for our furry friends is the fact that every canine is born equipped with powerful jaws and neck muscles for the specific purpose of being able to pull down and tear apart his hunted prey.

The structure of the jaw of every canine is such that it opens widely to hold large pieces of meat and bone, while the mechanics of a dog's jaw permits only vertical (up and down) movement that is designed for crushing.

The Canine Digestive Tract

A dog's digestive tract is short and simple and designed to move his natural choice of food (hide, meat and bone) quickly through his system.

The canine digestive system is simply unable to properly break down vegetable matter, which is why whole vegetables look pretty much the same going into your dog as they do coming out the other end.

Given the choice, most dogs would never choose to eat plants and grains or vegetables and fruits over meat; however, we humans continue to feed them a kibble-based diet that contains high amounts of vegetables, fruits and grains with low amounts of meat. Part of this is because we've been taught that it's a healthy, balanced diet for humans, and so we believe that it must be the same for our dogs. And the other part is because all the fillers in dog food are less expensive and easier on the budget.

How much healthier and long lived might our beloved Cavapoo be if instead of largely ignoring nature's design for our canine companions, we chose to feed them whole, unprocessed, species-appropriate food with the main ingredient being meat?

Whatever you decide to feed your dog, keep in mind that just as too much wheat, other grains and fillers in our human diet is having a detrimental effect on our health, the same can be very true for our best fur friends.

Our dogs are also suffering from many of the same life-threatening diseases that are rampant in our human society as a direct result of consuming a diet high in genetically altered, impure, processed and packaged foods.

The BARF Diet

Raw feeding advocates believe that the ideal diet for their dog is one that would be very similar to what a dog living in the wild would have access to, and these canine guardians are often opposed to feeding their dog any sort of commercially manufactured pet foods.

On the other hand, those opposed to feeding their dogs a raw or Biologically Appropriate Raw Food (BARF) diet believe that the risks associated with food-borne illnesses during the handling and feeding of raw meats outweigh the purported benefits.

Raw meats purchased at your local grocery store contain a much higher level of acceptable bacteria than raw food produced for dogs, because the meat purchased for human consumption is meant to be cooked, which will kill any bacteria.

This means that canine guardians feeding their dogs a raw food diet can be quite certain that commercially prepared raw foods sold in pet stores will be safer than raw meats purchased in grocery stores.

Many guardians of high-energy, working breed dogs will agree that their dogs thrive on a raw or BARF diet and strongly believe that the potential benefits of feeding a dog a raw food diet are many, including:

• Healthy, shiny coats
• Decreased shedding
• Fewer allergy problems
• Healthier skin
• Cleaner teeth
• Fresher breath
• Higher energy levels
• Improved digestion
• Smaller stools
• Strengthened immune system

- Increased mobility in arthritic pets
- General increase or improvement in overall health

All dogs, whether working breed or lap dogs, are amazing athletes in their own right; therefore, every dog deserves to be fed the best food available.

A raw diet is a direct evolution of what dogs ate before they became our domesticated pets and turned toward commercially prepared, easy-to-serve dry dog food that required no special storage or preparation.

The Dehydrated Diet

Dehydrated dog food comes in both raw and cooked forms, and these foods are usually air-dried to reduce moisture to the level where bacterial growth is inhibited.

The appearance of dehydrated dog food is very similar to dry kibble, and the typical feeding methods include adding warm water before serving, which makes this type of diet both healthy for our dogs and convenient for us to serve.

Dehydrated recipes are made from minimally processed fresh whole foods to create a healthy and nutritionally balanced meal that will meet or exceed the dietary requirements for healthy canines.

Dehydrating removes only the moisture from the fresh ingredients, which usually means that because the food has not already been cooked at a high temperature, more of the overall nutrition is retained.

A dehydrated diet is a convenient way to feed your dog a nutritious diet, because all you have to do is add warm water and wait five minutes while the food re-hydrates so your Cavapoo can enjoy a warm meal.

The Kibble Diet

While many canine guardians are starting to take a closer look at the food choices they are making for their furry companions, there is no mistaking that the convenience and relative economy of dry dog food kibble, which had its beginnings in the 1940s, continues to be the most popular pet food choice for most humans.

Photo Credit: Terri Schnieders of Willowbrook Cavaliers

While feeding a high-quality, bagged kibble diet that has been flavored to appeal to dogs and supplemented with vegetables and fruits to appeal to humans may keep most every Cavapoo companion happy and healthy, you will need to decide whether this is the best diet for them.

The First Lessons

Do not give a puppy full run of the house until the dog is housebroken. Use a baby gate to keep your pet in a controlled area, both to protect the puppy and your home. There are all kinds of hazards in your environment (like staircases and landings) that, while normal for you to navigate, are dangerous for a little dog.

Baby gates, depending on size and configuration, sell in a range of $25-$100 / £14.87-£59.46.

Any time you leave the house, put the puppy in his crate until you return.

Housebreaking

Cavapoos are generally easy to potty train. Even so, it can take several months for a dog to develop the required bladder control to be truly house trained. Dogs vary when it comes to how quickly they pick up potty training, so try not to put a time limit on the process. Also, don't be surprised by the occasional accident even after you think you've finished potty training.

The speed of potty training is affected by how consistent you and your family are. If every family member takes the puppy outside when he is showing signs of needing the toilet, progress will be much faster. However, this does require watching the puppy at all times.

A simple method for potty training a Cavapoo is as follows:

1.   Start by becoming familiar with your Cavapoo's toilet habits. At eight weeks old, a puppy is likely to need to go every

one or two hours. This might sound like a lot, but fortunately puppies develop bladder control quickly.

2.   Next, keep in mind that your puppy will need to go to the toilet soon after eating a meal. Create a schedule and take the dog outside when you think it needs to go. By pre-empting toileting you can eliminate many mistakes.

3.   Whenever you see a sign that your dog is about to go to the toilet, take him outside quickly. Warnings include sniffing the floor, walking in circles and unfocused eyes. If you're fast enough, it's best to let your dog walk outside rather than carrying him. Take the dog to the spot you want him to use as a toilet and give plenty of praise for successful toileting.

4.   Your crate can be a lifesaver when you have to leave your puppy alone. Once you've trained the puppy to be comfortable in a crate, he will see it as a "den" and won't want to soil it. Don't push the limits, as puppies have small bladders and become distressed when forced to use the crate as a toilet.

5.   Accidents are going to happen during potty training. Whenever your dog toilets on the floor, use a specialist cleaning product to remove the smell. This prevents the dog from associating an indoor area as a toilet.

Nature's Miracle Stain and Odor Removal is an excellent and affordable enzymatic cleaner at just $5 / £2.97 per 32 ounce / 0.9 liter bottle.

Always avoid getting angry or shouting during potty training. Cavapoo puppies are intelligent dogs and nearly always get the hang of potty training with consistent practice.

Additionally, never rub your puppy's nose in its waste after an accident. This doesn't work for any dog, especially those which respond best to positive reinforcement, and can cause the puppy to become scared without teaching why the punishment happened.

The following are methods that you may or may not have considered, all of which have their own merits, including:

• Bell training
• Exercise pen training
• Free training
• Kennel training

All of these are effective methods, so long as you add in the one critical and often missing "wild card" ingredient, which is "human training."

When you bring home your new Cavapoo puppy, he will be relying upon your guidance to teach him what he needs to learn. When it comes to housetraining, the first thing the human guardian needs to learn is that the puppy is not being bad when he pees or poops inside.

He is just responding to the call of Mother Nature, and you need to pay close attention right from the very beginning, because it's entirely possible to teach a puppy to go to the bathroom outside in less than a week. Therefore, if your puppy is making bathroom "mistakes," blame yourself, not your puppy.

Check in with yourself and make sure your energy remains consistently calm and patient and that you exercise plenty of compassion and understanding while you help your new puppy learn the bathroom rules. Don't clean up after your puppy while he is watching, as this makes the puppy believe you are there to clean up after him, making you lower in the dog pack order.

During the early stages of potty training, adding treats as an extra incentive can be a good way to reinforce how happy you are that your puppy is learning to relieve himself in the right place. Slowly, treats can be removed and replaced with your happy praise, or you can give your puppy a treat after they are back inside.

Next, now that you have a new puppy in your life, you will want to be flexible with respect to adapting your schedule to meet his internal clock. This will quickly teach your Cavapoo puppy his new bathroom routine.

This means not leaving your puppy alone for endless hours of time because he is a pack animal that needs constant companionship and direction. Long periods of time alone will result in the disruption of the potty training schedule you have worked hard to establish.

If you have no choice but to leave your puppy alone for many hours, make sure that you place him in a paper-lined room or pen where he can relieve himself without destroying your newly installed hardwood or favorite carpet.

Remember, your Cavapoo is a growing puppy with a bladder and bowels that they do not yet have complete control over.

Bell Training

A very easy way to introduce your new Cavapoo puppy to house training is to begin by teaching him how to ring a bell whenever he needs to go outside. A further benefit of training your puppy to ring a bell is that you will not have to listen to your puppy or dog whining, barking or howling to be let out, and your door will not become scratched from your puppy's nails.

Attach the bell to a piece of ribbon or string that hangs from a door handle or tape it to a doorsill where you will be taking your puppy out to toilet. The string will need to be long enough so that your puppy can easily reach the bell with his nose or a paw.

Next, each time you take your puppy out to relieve himself, say the word "outside potty," and use his paw or his nose to ring the bell. Praise him for this "trick" and immediately take him outside. This type of an alert system is an easy way to eliminate accidents in the home.

Photo Credit: Cindi Stump of Stump Farm Puppies Too

Kennel Training

When you train your Cavapoo puppy to accept sleeping in his own crate at night, this will also help to accelerate potty training. Since your puppy won't want to relieve himself where he sleeps, he will hold his bladder and bowels as long as he possibly can.

Presenting him with familiar scents by taking him to the same spot in the yard or the same street corner will help to remind and encourage him that he is outside to relieve himself.

Use a voice cue to remind your puppy why he is outside, such as "go pee," and always remember to praise him every time he relieves himself in the right place so that he quickly understands what you expect of him.

Exercise Pen Training

The exercise pen is a transition from crate training and will be helpful for those times when you may have to leave your Cavapoo puppy for more hours than he can reasonably be expected to wait to be let out.

Exercise pens are usually constructed of wire sections that can put together in whatever shape you desire. The pen needs to be large enough to hold your puppy's kennel in one half of the pen, while the other half will be lined with newspapers or pee pads.

Place your Cavapoo puppy's food and water dishes next to the crate and leave the door open (or take it off), so he can wander in and out whenever he wishes to eat or drink or go to the papers or pee pads if he needs to relieve himself.

Because he is already used to sleeping inside his kennel, he will not want to relieve himself inside the area where he sleeps; therefore, your puppy will naturally go to the other half of the pen to relieve himself on the newspapers or pee pads.

Free Training

If you would rather not confine your young Cavapoo puppy to one or two rooms in your home and will be allowing him to freely range about your home anywhere he wishes during the day, this is considered free training.

Never get upset or scold a puppy for having an accident inside the home, because this will result in teaching your puppy to be afraid of you and to only relieve himself in secret places or when you're not watching. If you catch your Cavapoo puppy making a mistake, all that is necessary is for you to calmly say "no" and quickly scoop him up and take him outside.

Cavapoos are not difficult to housebreak. They will generally do very well when you start them off with "puppy pee pads" that you will move closer and closer to the same door you always use when taking them outside. This way, they will quickly learn to associate going to this door when they need to relieve themselves.

Grooming

Do not allow yourself to get caught in the "my Cavapoo doesn't like it" trap, which is an excuse many owners will use to avoid regular grooming sessions. When you allow your Cavapoo to dictate whether he will permit a grooming session, you are setting a dangerous precedent.

Once you have bonded with your dog, they love to be tickled, rubbed and scratched in certain favorite places. This is why grooming is a great source of pleasure and a way to bond.

The Cavapoo doesn't require extensive grooming, but there are a few areas that need to be groomed either daily or at least a few times per week.

The Cavapoo has a thick coat that may or may not be curly. The coat can become matted quickly. For this reason, it's important to brush a Cavapoo regularly to prevent tangling.

Cavapoos that have inherited the Poodle's coat usually require more grooming, as the hair becomes matted faster. You should also be prepared to pay for professional coat grooming each month - most Cavapoo owners do this.

Laura Koch of Petit Jean Puppies has some tips: "The puppy coat is fairly easy but during the coat transition from puppy to adult, there seems to be a period of matting caused by the baby coat that's being shed and it needs to be removed by using a firm slicker brush. Regular maintenance brushing works best with a soft slicker brush. The easiest coat to keep is the straight sparse coat but it does shed more than the curlier coats. The F1b curliest coat is very easy to maintain but requires more grooming by a professional by clipping it back shorter."

Cavapoos usually love attention and are also fond of treats. This makes it easy to train a Cavapoo to enjoy being groomed. If you practice touching and brushing your dog from a young age, while using treats to reinforce that grooming is fun, older Cavapoos can be relatively easy to groom.

Brushing sessions are also a great chance to examine your pet's skin for any unusual growths, lumps, bumps or wounds. Be sure to check around the eyes, in and behind the ears, and around the mouth.

Aside from brushing the coat, it's a good idea to trim the area around the genitals and anus. The Cavapoo has a beautiful coat, but it can quickly become stained or start to smell without trimming these areas.

Danna Colman shares this tip: "I was always struggling with matts because Georgia's hair is very curly and dense. She really disliked any brushing or combing, so I would hardly groom her myself and just wait for her monthly professional grooming. A friend in England told me about this wonderful product called the Tangle Teezer. Actually, I believe it's for women's hair, but it works like a charm on Georgia because her hair is very similar to mine. Brushing now is fun and relaxing because Georgia believes she is getting a massage."

The Cavapoo's eyes, like Cavalier's, often run. This causes brown stains below the eyes. These should be cleaned daily to avoid irritation. Fortunately, the stains are often easy to remove with a wet flannel.

An area of the Cavapoo that requires extra attention is the ears. The Cavapoo has long ears that hang down. This can increase the chances of bacteria build-up and infection. You should check your Cavapoo's ears regularly and clean them when required.

If you do work with a professional groomer, find one who has experience with Cavapoos. Expect, on average, to pay $35-$60 / £30-£45 per session.

How to Bathe Your Cavapoo

A Cavapoo should be bathed between professional grooming appointments. This helps to keep the coat clean and soft. Bathing also reduces the chance of tangles.

The earlier you start bathing your Cavapoo, the easier it is going to be. If your Cavapoo gets used to it as a puppy, then he will be less difficult to handle later. Follow these tips:

1.)   Fill a bathtub with several inches of warm water.
2.)   Place your Cavapoo in the tub and wet down his coat.
3.)   Apply a dollop of dog shampoo to your hands and work it into your Cavapoo's coat, starting at the base of his neck.
4.)   Work the shampoo into your dog's back and down his legs and tail.

5.)   Rinse your dog well, getting rid of all the soap.

6.)   Towel dry to remove as much moisture as possible.

7.)   If desired, use a hair dryer on the cool setting to dry your Cavapoo's coat the rest of the way.

It is very important that you avoid getting water in your Cavapoo's ears and eyes. If your Cavapoo's ears get wet, dry them carefully with a cotton ball to prevent infection.

TIP: Try using Chamois cloths to dry your Cavapoo. It works great, and they don't have to be laundered as much. They just air dry and can be washed in the washing machine. However, DO NOT put the Chamois in the dryer. I have found that they work much better than towels.

Photo Credit: Kirstin Pollington of Milky Paws

Nail Trimming

Most Cavapoos do not like to have their nails trimmed as they have sensitive nails, but this is a regular bit of maintenance that cannot be ignored. Their nails should be kept as short as possible. That procedure should start at a very young age since they do not like their feet touched. Start early and do it weekly. They do best without tight restraint.

Depending on your dog's reaction, you can perform this chore yourself with an appropriate clipper. I prefer models with plier grips for ease of handling. Most brands sell for less than $20 / £11.88.

Even better than a nail clipper is the electric Dremel tool, since there is a lesser chance of cutting into the quick. In addition, your dog's nails will be smooth, without the sharp edges clipping alone can create.

NOTE: never use a regular Dremel™ tool, as it will be too high speed and will burn your dog's toenails. Only use a slow speed Dremel™, such as Model 7300-PT Pet Nail Grooming Tool (approx. $40/£20). You can also purchase the flexible hose attachment for the Dremel which is much easier to handle and can be held like a pencil.

Position your Cavapoo on an elevated surface. You need good visibility and working room. Don't be surprised if you have to ask someone to help you. The goal is to snip off the tip of each nail at a 45-degree angle. Be careful not to cut into the vascular quick at the base. You'll hurt the dog and the nail will bleed heavily.

If your Cavapoo absolutely refuses to cooperate, which is a real possibility, you may need to have your pet's nails trimmed at the vet's or by a professional groomer.

Fleas and Ticks

Fleas and ticks are often detected on a dog during grooming. While no one wants "passengers" on their pet, the occasional flea is just pretty much part of living your life with a dog. It happens. Deal with it. Move on.

Never put a commercial flea product on a puppy of less than 12 weeks of age and only use such products on adult dogs with extreme caution. The major flea control brands contain pyrethrum, which has been linked to long-term neurological damage. The chemical can be deadly for small dogs. Instead, use a standard canine shampoo and warm water. Bathe your dog and use a fine-toothed flea comb to work through the coat and trap the fleas. Kill the live fleas by submerging the comb in hot soapy water.

Wash all of the dog's bedding and any soft materials with which he has come in contact. Check all areas of the house where the dog sleeps for accumulations of "flea dirt," which is dried blood excreted by adult fleas. Make sure that there are no remaining eggs that will hatch and re-infest the dog, by washing these materials and surfaces daily for at least a week.

For ticks, coat the parasite with a thick layer of petroleum jelly and wait 5 minutes. The tick will suffocate and its jaw will release, allowing you to pluck it away from the skin with a straight motion using a pair of tweezers. Don't jerk the tick off! The head will stay in place and, if the tick is still alive, continue to burrow into the skin creating a painful sore.

Anal Glands

Blocked anal glands are common in dogs, evidenced by telltale scooting of the backside on the carpet or ground and a strong, foul odor. The blockage can only be relieved by expressing the glands. Unless this is done, an abscess may form. The delicate nature of this procedure should be left to a groomer or performed in the vet's office.

Collar or Harness?

As a staple of dog ownership, the traditional collar that fits around the neck is almost iconic, but I don't like this arrangement. I wouldn't want to go through life with something around my neck (especially with a leash attached) that with the mildest tug can create a choking sensation.

I prefer the on-body harness restraints that look like vests and offer a point of attachment between the dog's shoulders. The positioning affords excellent control without placing pressure on the neck. Young dogs accept these harnesses very well and are less likely to strain on the lead during walks.

Take your dog with you to get the best fit since sizing is difficult to guess. I've seen dogs as large as 14 lbs. / 6.35 kg take an "Extra Small." The fit really depends on build, more than weight. Most of these harnesses, regardless of size, sell for $20 - $25 / £11.88 - £14.85.

Standard Leash or Retractable?

Leash type is really a matter of personal preference. I use both fixed and retractable leads. Some facilities, like groomers, vet clinics, and dog daycares won't allow retractable because they create a trip-and-fall hazard for other human clients. Fixed length leashes sell for as little as $5 / £2.97, while retractable leads are priced under $15 / £8.91.

Any young dog has to learn to respect the leash. You do not create this respect by jerking or dragging at the lead. When he does that, pick him up, move to a new position, and start the walk over again. You must always convey that you are the one in charge. It's always best if your pet associates the lead with a positive adventure out in the world, but you have to stay in the driver's seat.

Reinforce good behavior on walks by praising your pet and offering him treats as a reward for obedience. As part of the routine, teach your Cavapoo to sit by issuing the command and simultaneously pointing down. Do not attach the lead to the harness until the dog obeys. Wait several seconds and then start the walk. If your dog jerks or pulls at the leash, stop, pick up your pet, and start over from the sit command.

The Importance of Basic Commands

Any young dog will benefit from attending a basic obedience class. Although stubborn, a Cavapoo, like any dog, is eager to please his master. That's simply the nature of a pack animal. If you give your dog consistent direction and a clear command language, you will have much greater success with training.

Cavapoos have the ability to assimilate about 165-200 words. They cannot, however, attach more than one meaning to any of those words. You must use the same command if you expect the same desirable response. If your dog barks, tell him to be "quiet." If he picks something up, say "drop it." For problem jumping, tell him to get "off." Pick a set of words and stick with them, using a tone of clear authority.

Many big box pet stores have trainers that conduct evening obedience classes. This is an excellent socialization opportunity as well as a means to gain some basic education for yourself and your pet. Start these lessons early, and you should have an extremely well-mannered companion.

Play Time and Tricks

In teaching any dog tricks, play to a natural tendency the dog displays and then work to extend and change the behavior until it becomes a "trick."

In selecting toys, don't choose any soft item that can be easily shredded, especially those made of rubber. If your pet swallows the pieces, the dog can choke or develop an intestinal blockage. Stay away from toys with "squeakers." Nylabones are a tried and true favorite and they are inexpensive at $1-$5 / £0.59-£2.97 range.

Photo Credit: Windie Sturges of Calla Lily Cavapoo

Don't give your Cavapoo rawhide or pig's ears. Both soften and present a choking hazard. Also avoid cow hooves. They splinter and could puncture the cheek or palate.

Playtime is important, especially for a dog's natural desire to chase. Try channeling this instinct with toys and games. If a dog has no stimulation and has nothing to chase, he can start to chase his own tail, which can lead to problems.

Toys can be used to simulate the dog's natural desire to hunt. For example, when he catches a toy, he will often shake it and bury his teeth into it, simulating the killing of their prey.

Allow your dog to fulfill a natural desire to chew. This comes from historically catching their prey and then chewing the carcass. Providing chews or bones can prevent your dog from destroying your home.

Playing with your dog is not only a great way of getting him to use up his energy, but it is also a great way of bonding with him as he has fun. Dogs love to chase and catch balls, just make sure that the ball is too large to be swallowed.

Deer antlers are wonderful toys for Cavapoos. Most love them. They do not smell, are all-natural and do not stain or splinter. I recommend the antlers that are not split as they last longer.

Dogs that don't get enough exercise are also more likely to develop problem behaviors like chewing, digging and barking.

Laura Koch of Petit Jean Puppies advises: "I've noticed that when the pups start getting their molars, they go through a vigorous chewing phase that needs to be monitored closely. What once took them a month to chew through can now take just an hour. I've had several people had to rush their pup to the emergency clinic because of chewing bully sticks too fast resulting in vomiting and diarrhea. Nylabones, Kongs and Antlers seem to be the safest."

Chapter 6 - Training and Problem Behaviors

Training a Cavapoo can be a lot of fun. Cavapoos are usually willing to learn and want to please their owners. They also pick up commands and hand signals incredibly quickly. If you take your Cavapoo to a training class, your puppy will probably be one of the fastest to learn commands such as "sit" and "stay."

Photo Credit: Kristin Pollington of Milky Paws

When most new dog owners imagine training a Cavapoo puppy, they often think of teaching specific commands. It's true that commands are important and could even save your dog's life one day, but most training takes place outside of training sessions. As professional dog trainers know, every interaction between a dog and owner is an opportunity for training.

Cavapoos and Bad Habits

The hardest part about training a Cavapoo is preventing bad habits. Cavapoo puppies are cute and full of personality, which means they often get away with bad behaviors. Who doesn't want an excited, fluffy puppy leaping into their lap? Or to be licked all over by an adorable Cavapoo? The problem is that these behaviors aren't so cute when the dog is fully grown, and they often get more extreme over time.

It's sometimes difficult to persuade friends, family and even strangers that behaviors such as jumping up, mouthing and excessive licking are not acceptable. This can lead to continuous reinforcement of behaviors you don't want to encourage.

So how can you prevent bad habits? Firstly, you should never punish your puppy. Punishment isn't effective as a training method, and it can damage the bond between you and your Cavapoo. The Cavapoo is often a confident breed, but it doesn't cope well with negative training methods. This is especially true for physical punishment such as hitting.

If your dog does something that is unacceptable, such as jumping up, ignore him. Even if you find it difficult to resist those cute Cavapoo eyes, the simple act of looking at him is often enough to make him associate the behavior with attention. Shouting at the dog also doesn't work, especially to prevent barking. The dog is likely to think you're talking back to it!

If the behavior just can't be ignored – biting your legs, for example – gently correct the dog and carry on with what you are doing. This might take some repetition, but the puppy will eventually get the message.

Training a Cavapoo – or any dog – often comes back to consistency. If you consistently discourage bad behaviors from the moment you bring your puppy home, the dog grows up knowing exactly what is allowed. On the other hand, if you allow your puppy to jump up when you get home from work – even if most of the time you discourage it - bad habits are likely to form.

Training a Cavapoo to Respond to Commands

Treats are extremely useful once you start training commands such as "sit" and "leave it." While some dogs aren't interested in treats, Cavapoos usually love them. To start with, you should give a treat every time your dog completes a command successfully.

Once the puppy starts to understand a command, only give a treat occasionally rather than every time. This prevents the puppy from obeying only when a treat is involved. It also reduces the chances of the puppy becoming overweight – a common problem for Cavapoos due to their love of treats.

Also, keep in mind that dogs don't naturally generalize commands to different locations. A dog that's trained to "sit" inside may not understand "sit" on a walk. If your Cavapoo doesn't respond to your command, whether this is because it is distracted or just doesn't seem to want to, this is usually because it isn't fully trained in every location.

The best way to train a command is to practice in increasingly difficult situations. Training your dog to "come" when in your house, for example, doesn't mean the command will be followed when on a walk. You need to train your dog to "come" indoors, in the yard, on walks and any other location so that your dog always responds. This takes time, but Cavapoos are quick to learn.

Enroll your pet in a training class and expose him to new sights, sounds, people and places. Be attentive to the behavior of your own dog as well as what's going on around you. Often in a public setting the best way to ensure there are no problems is to avoid other dogs altogether — not because your pet can't behave, but because another dog owner isn't in control of his animal.

Dog Whispering

Many people can be confused when they need professional help with their dog, because for many years, if you needed help with your dog, you contacted a "dog trainer" or took your dog to "puppy classes" where your dog would learn how to sit or stay.

The difference between a dog trainer and a dog whisperer would be that a "dog trainer" teaches a dog how to perform certain tasks, and a "dog whisperer" alleviates behavior problems by teaching humans what they need to do to keep their particular dog happy.

Often, depending on how soon the guardian has sought help, this can mean that the dog in question has developed some pretty serious issues, such as aggressive barking, lunging, biting or attacking other dogs, pets or people.

Dog whispering is often an emotional roller coaster ride for the guardian, as he finally realizes that it has been his actions (or inactions) that have likely caused the unbalanced behavior that the dog has been displaying.

Once solutions are provided, the relief for both dog and human can be quite cathartic when they realize that with the correct direction, they can indeed live a happy life with their dog.

All specific methods of training, such as "clicker training," fall outside of what every dog needs to be happy. Training your dog to respond to a clicker (which you can easily do on your own) and then letting him sleep in your bed, eat from your plate and any other multitude of things humans allow, are what makes the dog unbalanced and causes behavior problems.

I always tell people not to wait until there is a severe problem before getting some dog whispering or professional help of some sort, because with the proper training, man can learn to be dog's best friend.

Photo Credit: Rebecca Posten of Riverside Puppies

Teaching Basic Commands

When it comes to training your Cavapoo, you have to start off slowly with the basic commands. The most popular basic commands for dogs include sit, down, stay and come.

Sit

This is the most basic and one of the most important commands you can teach your Cavapoo.

1.) Stand in front of your Cavapoo with a few small treats in your pocket.

2.) Hold one treat in your dominant hand and wave it in front of your Cavapoo's nose so he gets the scent.

3.) Give the "Sit" command.

4.) Move the treat upward and backward over your Cavapoo's head so he is forced to raise his head to follow it.

5.) In the process, his bottom will lower to the ground.

6.) As soon as your Cavapoo's bottom hits the ground, praise him and give him the treat.

7.) Repeat this process several times until your Cavapoo gets the hang of it and responds consistently.

Down

After the "Sit" command, "Down" is the next logical command to teach because it is a progression from "Sit."

1.)   Kneel in front of your Cavapoo with a few small treats in your pocket.

2.)   Hold one treat in your dominant hand and give your Cavapoo the "Sit" command.

3.)   Reward your Cavapoo for sitting, then give him the "Down" command.

4.)   Quickly move the treat down to the floor between your Cavapoo's paws.

5.)   Your Cavapoo will follow the treat and should lie down to retrieve it.

6.)   Praise and reward your Cavapoo when he lies down.

7.)   Repeat this process several times until your Cavapoo gets the hang of it and responds consistently.

Come

It is very important that your Cavapoo responds to a "come" command, because there may come a time when you need to get his attention and call him to your side during a dangerous situation (such as him running around too close to traffic).

1.)   Put your Cavapoo on a short leash and stand in front of him.

2.)   Give your Cavapoo the "Come" command, then quickly take a few steps backward away from him.

3.)   Clap your hands and act excited, but do not repeat the "Come" command.

4.)   Keep moving backwards in small steps until your Cavapoo follows and comes to you.

5.)   Praise and reward your Cavapoo and repeat the process.

6.)   Over time, you can use a longer leash or take your Cavapoo off the leash entirely.

7.)   You can also start by standing further from your Cavapoo when you give the "Come" command.

8.)   If your Cavapoo doesn't come to you immediately, you can use the leash to pull him toward you.

Stay

This command is very important because it teaches your Cavapoo discipline. Not only does it teach your Cavapoo to stay, but it also forces him to listen and pay attention to you.

1.)   Find a friend to help you with this training session.

2.)   Have your friend hold your Cavapoo on the leash while you stand in front of the dog.

3.)   Give your Cavapoo the "Sit" command and reward him for responding correctly.

4.)   Give your dog the "Stay" command while holding your hand out like a "Stop" sign.

5.)   Take a few steps backward away from your dog and pause for 1 to 2 seconds.

6.)   Step back toward your Cavapoo, then praise and reward your dog.

7.)   Repeat the process several times, and then start moving back a little farther before you return to your Cavapoo.

Beyond Basic Training

Once your Cavapoo has a firm grasp on the basics, you can move on to teaching him additional commands. You can also add distractions to the equation to reinforce your dog's mastery of the commands. The end goal is to ensure that your Cavapoo responds to your command each and every time, regardless of distractions and anything else he might rather be doing. This is incredibly important, because there may come a time when your dog is in a dangerous situation, and if he doesn't respond to your command, he could get hurt.

After your Cavapoo has started to respond correctly to the basic commands on a regular basis, you can start to incorporate distractions.

If you previously conducted your training sessions indoors, you might consider moving them outside where your dog could be distracted by various sights, smells and sounds.

One thing you might try is to give your dog the Stay command and then toss a toy nearby that will tempt him to break his Stay. Start by tossing the toy at a good distance from him and wait a few seconds before you release him to play.

Eventually you will be able to toss a toy right next to your dog without him breaking his Stay until you give him permission to do so.

Incorporating Hand Signals

Teaching your Cavapoo to respond to hand signals in addition to verbal commands is very useful, as you never know when the occasion might arise when your dog is unable to hear you.

To start out, choose your dominant hand to give the hand signals and hold a small treat in that hand while you are training your dog. This will encourage your dog to focus on your hand during training, and it will help to cement the connection between the command and the hand signal.

To begin, give your dog the Sit or Down command while holding the treat in your dominant hand and give the appropriate hand signal. For Sit you might try a closed fist, and for Down, you might place your hand flat and parallel to the ground.

Photo Credit: Paul & Michele Flower owner of Wally

When your dog responds correctly, give him the treat. You will need to repeat this process many times in order for your dog to form a connection between both the verbal command and the hand signal with the desired behavior.

Eventually, you can start to remove the verbal command from the equation. Use the hand gesture every time but start to use the verbal command only half the time.

Once your dog gets the hang of this, you should start to remove the food reward from the equation. Continue to give your dog the hand signal for each command, and occasionally use the verbal command just to remind him.

You should start to phase out the food rewards by offering them only half the time. Progressively lessen the use of the food reward but continue to praise your dog for performing the behavior correctly so he learns to repeat it.

Teaching Distance Commands

In addition to getting your dog to respond to hand signals, it is also useful to teach him to respond to your commands even when you are not directly next to him.

This may come in handy if your dog is running around outside and gets too close to the street. You should be able to give him a Sit or Down command so he stops before he gets into a dangerous situation.

Teaching your dog distance commands is not difficult, but it does require some time and patience.

To start, give your Cavapoo a brief refresher course of the basic commands while you are standing or kneeling right next to him.

Next, give your dog the Sit and Stay commands, then move a few feet away before you give the Come command.

Repeat this process, increasing the distance between you and your dog before giving him the Come command. Be sure to praise and reward him for responding appropriately when he does so.

Once your dog gets the hang of coming on command from a distance, you can start to incorporate other commands.

One method of doing so is to teach your dog to sit when you grab his collar. To do so, let your dog wander freely, and every once in a while walk up and grab his collar while giving the Sit command.

After a few repetitions, your dog should begin to respond with a Sit when you grab his collar, even if you do not give the command.

Gradually, you can increase the distance from which you come to grab his collar and give the command.

After your dog starts to respond consistently when you come from a distance to grab his collar, you can start giving the Sit command without moving toward him.

It may take your dog a few times to get the hang of it, so be patient. If your dog doesn't Sit right away, calmly walk up to him and repeat the Sit command but do not grab his collar this time. Eventually, your dog will get the hang of it, and you can start to practice using other commands like Down and Stay from a distance.

Clicker Training

When it comes to training your Cavapoo, you are going to be most successful if you maintain consistency. Unless you are very clear with your dog about what your expectations are, he may simply decide not to follow your commands.

A simple way to achieve consistency in training your Cavapoo is to use the principles of clicker training. Clicker training involves using a small handheld device that makes a clicking noise when you press it between your fingers.

Clicker training is based on the theory of operant conditioning, which helps your dog to make the connection between the desired behavior and the offering of a reward.

Cavapoos have a natural desire to please, so if they learn that a certain behavior earns your approval, they will be eager to repeat it. Clicker training is a great way to help your dog quickly identify the particular behavior you want him to repeat.

All you have to do is give your Cavapoo a command, and as soon as he performs the behavior, use the clicker. After you use the clicker, give your dog the reward as you would with any form of positive reinforcement training.

Some of the benefits of clicker training include:

• Very easy to implement – all you need is the clicker.
• Helps your dog form a connection between the command and the desired behavior more quickly.
• You only need to use the clicker until your dog makes the connection, then you can stop.
• May help to keep your dog's attention more effectively if he hears the noise.

Clicker training is just one method of positive reinforcement training that you can consider for training your Cavapoo.

No matter what method you choose, it is important that you maintain consistency and always praise and reward your dog for responding to your commands correctly so he learns to repeat the behavior.

First Tricks

In order to give your Cavapoo extra incentive while teaching him his first tricks, find a small treat that he would do anything to get, and give the treat as a reward to help solidify a good performance.

Most dogs will be extra attentive during training sessions when they know that they will be rewarded with their favorite treats.

Photo Credit: Honey by Charlotte G Photography

If your Cavapoo is less than six months old when you begin teaching him tricks, keep your training sessions short (no more than 5 or 10 minutes) and make the sessions lots of fun.

You can extend your training sessions once your Cavapoo becomes an adult because he will be able to maintain focus for longer periods of time.

Shake a Paw

Who doesn't love a dog who knows how to shake a paw? This is one of the easiest tricks to teach your Cavapoo.

Practice every day until your Cavapoo is 100% reliable with this trick, and then it will be time to add another trick to the repertoire.

Most dogs are naturally either right or left pawed. If you know which paw your dog favors, ask him to shake this paw.

Find a quiet place to practice, without noisy distractions or other pets, and stand or sit in front of your dog. Place him in the sitting position and hold a treat in your left hand.

Say the command "Shake" while putting your right hand behind his left or right paw and pull the paw gently toward you until you are holding his paw in your hand. Immediately praise and give him the treat.

Most dogs will learn the "Shake" trick very quickly, and in no time at all, once you put out your hand, your Cavapoo will immediately lift his paw and put it into your hand without your assistance or any verbal cue.

Roll Over

You will find that just like your Cavapoo is naturally either right or left pawed, he will also naturally want to roll either to the right or the left side. Take advantage of this by asking your dog to roll to the side he naturally prefers. Sit with your dog on the floor and put him in a lie down position.

Hold a treat in your hand and place it close to your Cavapoo's nose without allowing him to grab it. While he is in the lying position, move the treat to the right or left side of his head so he has to roll over to get to it.

You will quickly see which side your Cavapoo naturally rolls. Once you see this, move the treat to that side. Once he rolls over to that side, immediately give him the treat and praise him.

You can say the verbal cue "Over" while demonstrating the hand signal motion (moving your right hand in a half circular motion) from one side of your Cavapoo's head to the other.

Sit Pretty

Although this trick does require balance and is a little more complicated, most dogs pick up on it very quickly. Be sure to always exercise patience.

Find a quiet space with few distractions and sit or stand in front of your dog and ask him to "Sit."

Have a treat nearby on a countertop or table, and when your Cavapoo sits, use both hands to lift up his front paws into the sitting pretty position while saying the command "Sit Pretty." Help him balance while you praise and give him the treat.

Once your Cavapoo can do the balancing part of the trick quite easily without your help, sit or stand in front of your dog while asking him to "Sit Pretty" and hold the treat above his head at the level his nose would be when sitting pretty.

If your Cavapoo attempts to stand on his back legs to get the treat, you may be holding the treat too high, which will encourage him to stand up on his back legs to reach it. Go back to the first step and put him back into the "Sit" position and again lift his paws while his backside remains on the floor.

The hand signal for "Sit Pretty" is a straight arm held over your dog's head with a closed fist. Place him beside a wall when first teaching this trick so he can use the wall to help his balance.

A young Cavapoo puppy should be able to easily learn these basic tricks before he is six months old, and when you are patient and make your training sessions short and fun for your dog, he will be eager to learn more.

Photo Credit: Christy Shanklin of Christy's Puppies

Common Cavapoo Bad Behaviors

Some breeds of dogs are predisposed to certain bad behaviors. Other behaviors are learned, often without the owner realizing. Don't despair if your dog develops bad habits. Many behavioral issues can be eliminated with proper training.

If you buy a Cavapoo, the personality of the parent dogs will affect your puppy's behavior. Some of the most common bad behaviors associated with Cavapoos include:

Jumping Up

Jumping up often develops due to accidental reinforcement. A Cavapoo puppy jumping up is often considered cute, but a muddy and wet adult Cavapoo jumping up at a stranger on a walk certainly is a problem! For this reason it's important to teach a Cavapoo not to jump up from a young age.

When excessive jumping occurs, it may well be a dominance display or an example of amplifying separation anxiety. The dog may either see himself as higher in the pack hierarchy than you, or he may be trying to stop you from leaving the house.

Under all circumstances, be stern in enforcing the no jumping rule. If you are not, you will only confuse your pet. All dogs understand space as a concept. Don't retreat when a dog jumps, step into him and slightly to the side taking back the area he's trying to claim. You aren't trying to knock your pet down, but this may well happen if he forces the issue.

Your role is to move with slow deliberation and to stay casual, calm and confident. Control the "bubble" of space around your body, and don't let the dog invade that territory. The dog won't anticipate or like your response. It may take a few such encounters, but sending a dominant message will stop a jumper.

Barking Behavior

The amount a Cavapoo barks depends on its parents. Some Cavapoos will bark at the slightest noise in the house or garden, which can quickly become frustrating and a problem for neighbors. While barking isn't an issue for all Cavapoos, it should be discouraged from the moment you adopt a puppy. If you have a barker, you have to try to understand why your dog is making so much racket. Loneliness? Boredom? Excitement? Anxiety? Is he seeing, hearing, or smelling something? Has something changed that he perceives to be a threat?

Be firm and consistent with your admonitions. Some Cavapoo owners use a plant mister or squirt gun as negative reinforcement. Aim for the face, but don't let the stream of water hit the eyes. The only goal is to get your pet's attention and to create a negative association with the bad behavior.

Humane bark collars are also an option. These units release a harmless spray of citronella into the dog's nose triggered by vibrations from the animal's throat. Although somewhat expensive at $100/£60, the system works in almost all cases.

Digging

Digging is also an expression of fear, anxiety, and/or boredom. While trying to dig his way out and go find you, a determined and anxious digger will destroy furniture and claw through doors.

Again, increase the dog's exercise time. If giving your dog more attention doesn't work, consider taking your Cavapoo to a dog daycare facility so he won't be alone during the day.

Begging

Don't let begging get started in the first place, and you won't be faced with trying to stop the behavior! Make "people" food off limits from day one and don't cheat! If you have to take your dog to another part of the house while you are eating, do it. This isn't so much to control your pet as to control yourself. If you can't ignore a pleading set of Cavapoo eyes, you're the problem, not the dog!

Chewing

Although a natural behavior, chewing to excess is a sign of boredom and anxiety. The answer may be as simple as spending more time with your pet or getting him out of the house for longer periods of time. It's also important to direct the dog's chewing toward proper toys like Nylabones. Confiscate inappropriate items and reprimand the dog, offering him an acceptable chew toy instead.

Biting

Cavapoos are almost never aggressive and biting is rare, but they can learn to be defensive if they feel threatened or believe they are "pack leader." This behavior is sometimes called "small dog syndrome."

Young Cavapoos will often play bite more than other puppies, which should be discouraged. Mouthing, which is when a dog places teeth on the skin without applying any pressure, is another common behavior that is often an attempt to get attention. Gently curb this kind of rambunctious behavior. What is cute in a little puppy can be a disaster waiting to happen with an adult dog.

A dog bites as a means of primary defense and in reaction to fear or pain. Again, correct socialization will lessen the chances of a Cavapoo resorting to this behavior. If an adult dog does start to bite, get to the bottom of the issue quickly.

Begin with a trip to the vet because your Cavapoo may be in pain from an undiagnosed health problem. If that is not the case, enlist the services of a professional trainer immediately.

Photo Credit: Nicki Mannix owner of Bella

Territorial Marking

Any dog with an intact reproductive system, regardless of gender, will mark territory by urinating. In most cases this behavior occurs outdoors, but if the dog is upset about something, marking can also occur inside. Again, use an enzymatic cleaner to remove the odor. Otherwise, the dog may be attracted to use the same location again. Territorial marking occurs most frequently with intact males. As a long-term solution, have the dog neutered.

Do not think that territorial marking is caused by poor house training. The two behaviors are completely unrelated and driven by different reactions and urges.

Hyperactivity

Hyperactivity is another behavior that is often reinforced as a puppy. Every puppy has hyper moments, but Cavapoos are naturally energetic dogs. If a puppy gets attention for being overly excited, it is likely to continue the behavior as an adult. Most Cavapoos start to calm down after passing through adolescence, but this can take up to two years.

Separation Anxiety

Cavaliers and Poodles are both companion breeds, so it's not surprising that Cavapoos can often suffer from separation anxiety. A Cavapoo with separation anxiety will often bark, become destructive, toilet indoors (even after being potty trained) and drool excessively. Separation distress, which is less severe, is common among puppies but with the right training can be eliminated.

When your Cavapoo realizes you are about to leave the house, you may see behaviors like uncontrollable jumping or nervous cowering. The dog may begin to follow you around and do everything possible to get your attention as his discomfort escalates.

The best thing you can do to get ahead of separation anxiety from the beginning is to crate train your puppy. If a dog feels that he has a safe place, you have given him an essential coping mechanism against anxiety. Far from being a punishment, the crate is a comfort to your pet.

Chapter 7 – Cavapoo Health

When your Cavapoo needs to see his "primary care" physician, you'll take your pet to a vet. On a daily basis, however, you are your dog's real healthcare provider. As the years go by, you will know your Cavapoo better than anyone.

You will know what is normal. If you think something is wrong, even in the absence of obvious injury or illness, never hesitate to have your dog evaluated. The greater your understanding of preventive health care, the better you will be able to observe your pet and spot potential problems before they become serious.

Photo Credit: Danna Colman owner of Georgia

Your Veterinarian Is Your Partner

If you do not have an established relationship with a qualified veterinarian, get recommendations from your breeder or local dog club.

Always see the vet for the first time without your Cavapoo. Make it clear when you set up the appointment that you are there to meet the doctor, evaluate the clinic, and that you will pay for the visit. Veterinarians are busy people. Don't waste their time. Prepare your questions in advance and make sure to cover the following points:

- How long has this practice been in operation?
- How many vets are on staff?
- Are any of those doctors specialists? If so, in what area?
- Where do you refer patients if necessary?
- What are your regular hours? Emergency hours?
- Are you affiliated with an emergency clinic?
- What specific services does the clinic offer?
- Do you have or can you recommend a groomer?
- May I have an estimated schedule of fees?
- Do you currently treat any Cavapoos?

Pay attention to what you see and hear. You want to get a sense of the doctor, the facility and the staff. Look for:

- How the staff interacts with clients
- The visible level of organization
- Evidence of engagement with the clientele (office bulletin board, cards and photos displayed, etc.)
- The quality of all visible equipment
- The condition of the waiting area and back rooms
- Prominent display of doctors' credentials

Always go with your own "gut." You will know if the place "feels" right. Trust your intuition. If you don't like the "feel" of a clinic, even if it's modern and well-appointed, keep looking. If they make a comment that all Cavapoos are unhealthy or require eye and ear surgery, all have skin problems etc., LEAVE and find a vet without those pre-conceived notions.

Your Dog's First Visit to the Vet

When you choose a vet with whom you are comfortable, make a second appointment that will include your Cavapoo. Take the puppy's medical records with you. Routine procedures during the visit will include:

- Temperature
- Checking the heart and lungs with a stethoscope
- Weighing the dog
- Taking basic measurements to chart growth and physical progress

Be prepared to discuss completing your pet's vaccinations and scheduling the surgery to spay or neuter the dog. Write down any questions that occur to you before you get to the clinic!

Vaccinations

Recommended vaccinations begin at 6-7 weeks of age. The standard shots include:

- Distemper
- Hepatitis
- Parvovirus
- Parainfluenza
- Coronavirus

Boosters are set for 9, 12 and 16 weeks. In some areas a vaccine for Lyme disease starts at 16 weeks with a booster at 18 weeks. The rabies vaccination is administered at 12-16 weeks and then generally every 3 years.

Evaluating for Worms

It is extremely rare for a puppy acquired from a reputable breeder to have parasites. "Worms" are much more common in rescue dogs and strays. If present, roundworms appear as small white granules around the anus. Other types of worms can only be detected through a microscope.

Some parasites, like tapeworms, may be life threatening. Screening tests are important and do not reflect on your perceived care of the dog. If the puppy tests positive, the standard treatment is a deworming agent with a follow-up dose in 10 days.

It's best to take a stool sample at around 6-7 weeks to determine if the dog has worms or giardia. When the results are negative, it is not necessary to de-worm them. Some breeders just give them deworming medicine routinely. It's very important for a fecal sample to be obtained and sent to a recognized lab for testing.

Spaying and Neutering

The surgery reduces aggression and territoriality in males and reduces the risk of prostatic disease or perianal tumors. Neutered males are also less likely to mark territory or to behave inappropriately against the legs of your visitors.

Spaying eliminates hormonally related mood swings in females and protects them against uterine and ovarian cancer while lowering the risk for breast cancer.

(It is a complete myth that dogs that have been neutered are more likely to put on weight.)

"Normal" Health Issues

There are a number of health issues associated with Cavapoos, which we will discuss shortly under genetic abnormalities. All dogs can face "normal" health-related issues that may require the services of a vet, however, so we'll cover those first.

Any time that your pet seems inattentive or lethargic or stops eating and drinking, a trip to the vet is in order. None of these behaviors are normal for a healthy dog.

Photo Credit: Dawn Smith owner of Dughie-Doo

Diarrhea

All puppies are easily subject to upset stomachs for the simple reason that they get into things they shouldn't, like the kitchen garbage. Any case of diarrhea caused by such indiscriminate snooping should resolve within 24 hours. Give the dog smaller than normal portions of dry food, no treats, and plenty of fresh, clean water. Do not let the puppy become dehydrated. If the stools are still watery and loose after 24 hours, call the vet.

Use the same strategy of watchful waiting for adult dogs. When episodic diarrhea becomes chronic, it's time to re-evaluate your pet's diet in consultation with your veterinarian.

Dogs with chronic diarrhea are likely getting too much rich, fatty food. The diet will have to be adjusted to include less fat and protein. Some dogs also do better eating small amounts several times a day rather than having 2-3 larger meals.

Allergies may also be the hidden culprit behind chronic diarrhea. Allergies to chicken and turkey are particularly common. A change in diet resolves gastrointestinal upset due to allergies immediately. Many dogs do much better eating foods based on rabbit or duck.

Finally, dogs can suffer diarrhea from bacteria or viruses. If this is the case, your pet will also run a fever and vomit. In these cases, veterinary treatment is absolutely indicated.

Vomiting

Vomiting from an abrupt dietary change or from eating something inappropriate should also resolve within 24 hours. If your Cavapoo has unproductive vomiting, regurgitates blood, or can't keep water down, take him to the vet immediately

Dehydration from vomiting occurs faster than in a case of diarrhea and can be fatal. It is not unusual for a dog under these circumstances to require IV fluids.

Look around the area for anything the dog may have chewed and swallowed that triggered the vomiting. Identifying the culprit can be crucial in pinpointing the best treatment. Other possible causes include: hookworm, roundworm, pancreatitis, diabetes, thyroid disease, kidney disease, liver disease or a physical blockage.

General Signs of Illness

Dogs exhibiting any of the following symptoms should be evaluated by a vet. Never worry about being seen as an alarmist. Most problems can be resolved quickly if the dog is taken in for treatment at the first sign of illness.

Coughing and/or Wheezing

The occasional cough is no reason for concern, but if it lasts more than a week, your pet should be seen by the vet. A cough can be a symptom of:

- Kennel cough
- Heartworm
- Cardiac disease
- Bacterial infections
- Parasites
- Tumors
- Allergies

Kennel cough is an upper respiratory condition that is a form of canine bronchitis. It spreads quickly in poorly ventilated, overcrowded and warm conditions. The illness presents with a dry, hacking cough. Although kennel cough typically resolves on its own, your vet may suggest a cough suppressant and a humidifier to ease the irritation in your pet's airways.

For coughs of unknown origin, a full medical history will be taken and tests ordered. These will include X-rays and blood work. If necessary, fluid may be drawn from the lungs for additional analysis. It's always important to rule out heartworms as the causal agent.

Heartworms

Heartworms (*Dirofilaria Immitis*) are long, thin parasites spread through mosquito bites. The worms infest cardiac tissue, blocking the vessels that supply the heart and causing bleeding. If left untreated, they may cause heart failure.

Symptoms of a heartworm infestation include an intolerance to exercise, coughing and fainting. Discuss heartworm prevention with your vet who can advise you about the most effective preventative measures, including vaccines.

Other Warning Signs of Illness

Other warning signs of potential illness include:

- Unexplained, excessive drooling.
- Excessive consumption of water.
- Increased urination.
- Changes in appetite.
- Weight gain or loss.
- Marked change in levels of activity.
- Disinterest in favorite activities.
- Stiffness and difficulty standing or climbing stairs.
- Sleeping more than normal.
- Excessive shaking of the head (Cavapoos are head shakers even when healthy).
- Any sores, lumps or growths.
- Dry, red, or cloudy eyes.

Often the signs of serious illness are subtle. Trust your instincts. If you think something is wrong, do not hesitate to consult with your vet.

Diabetes

Three forms of diabetes are present in dogs: diabetes insipidus, diabetes mellitus and gestational diabetes. Each is caused by malfunctioning endocrine glands and may be linked to poor diet. Larger dogs are in a higher risk category.

- *Diabetes insipidus* - Low levels of the hormone vasopressin create problems with the regulation of blood glucose, salt and water.

- *Diabetes mellitus* - The most common and dangerous form, seen as Types I and II. Diabetes mellitus first develops in young dogs and may be referred to as "juvenile," while adult dogs most often suffer from Type II. All cases are treated with insulin.

- *Gestational diabetes* – This form occurs in pregnant females and requires the same treatment as diabetes mellitus. Obese dogs are at greater risk.

Blood sugar levels are affected by abnormal insulin production. Under the right conditions, such as being overweight, any mammalian species can develop diabetes.

Symptoms of Canine Diabetes

These following behaviors are signs that a dog may have canine diabetes:

- Excessive water consumption

- Frequent urination
- Lethargy / uncharacteristic laziness
- Weight gain or loss for no reason

In many cases, however, there are no evident symptoms. Diabetes comes on slowly. Its effects are not always immediately noticeable. Regular check-ups help to detect this disease before it becomes so serious as to be life threatening.

Photo Credit: Danna Colman owner of Georgia

Managing Diabetes

Managing canine diabetes typically includes the use of a special diet. Insulin injections may also be necessary. This may sound daunting, but anyone can learn to give the shots. Dogs with diabetes live full and normal lives; however, they will need to see the vet more often to monitor potential heart, eye and circulatory problems. In most cases the dog will develop diabetic cataracts and can go blind quickly. There is a surgery to remove diseased lens of the eyes and replace with artificial lenses that can restore sight.

Dental Care

Dogs maintain their teeth with chewing. If they don't get enough of this kind of activity, dental problems can develop early in life, including accumulated plaque and gum disease.

Often the first indication that something is wrong is severe bad breath. Usually gingivitis develops first. Left untreated, it can progress to actual periodontitis. Warning signs of gum disease include:

- Unwillingness to finish meals
- Extreme bad breath
- Swelling of the gums
- Bleeding gums
- Irregularities in the gum line
- Plaque build-up
- Drooling
- Loose teeth

Periodontitis is a bacterial infection. It causes inflammation, gum recession and possible tooth loss. In order to prevent the infection from spreading to other parts of the body, your vet will first prescribe a thorough cleaning, followed by a course of antibiotics. Symptoms include:

- Pus at the gum line
- Loss of appetite
- Depression
- Irritability
- Pawing at the mouth
- Trouble chewing

- Loose or missing teeth
- Gastrointestinal upset

During the course of the dental cleaning, other work may be required including, root canals, descaling and even extractions.

A dog can also suffer from an overgrowth of the gums called Proliferating Gum Disease, which is also a source of inflammation and infection. Other symptoms include:

- Thickening and lengthening of the gums
- Bleeding
- Bad breath
- Drooling
- Loss of appetite

Cleaning, surgery and antibiotics may all be required.

Home Dental Care

To get ahead of potential dental problems, there are numerous products you can use at home with your Cavapoo. Additives in the dog's water can help to break up tartar and plaque, but not all dogs can tolerate these mixtures without stomach upset. Dental sprays and wipes are an option, but gentle gum massage may be all that's needed to break up plaque and tartar.

Most owners use some kind of dental chew because it serves the dual purpose of being both preventive dental care and a dog treat.

The best protection for your dog's oral health is the same one you use — brushing, but with a canine-specific toothbrush and toothpaste. NEVER use human toothpaste. Fluoride, Xylitol and Aspertame used in human toothpaste are toxic to dogs.

Some canine toothbrushes are just smaller versions of the ones we use, but I prefer the brushes that just fit over the end of your finger. They offer terrific control and are easier to handle.

Like most things with a Cavapoo, the dog will either be completely cooperative or refuse to get onboard at all. There seems to be little middle ground with the breed on such issues. If you can get your dog comfortable having your hands in his mouth, the fingertip brushes are an unobtrusive addition to massaging the gums with just your fingers. Many vets say if you can simply manage to smear toothpaste on the animal's teeth, you're improving your pet's dental health.

Always try to brush the dog's teeth when he's a little tired and more likely to be cooperative. Don't do anything that will stress your pet. Use small circular motions. Stop if your pet seems to be getting antsy or annoyed. Better to spread a complete brushing out over two or three sessions than to create a negative association in your dog's mind.

Danna Colman shares this tip: "I have an excellent method for cleaning Georgia's teeth, and it's so easy! I tried toothbrushes, etc., and I never felt that her teeth were getting clean. I use an exfoliating glove. I just use my thumb and forefinger. I wet the tips and apply the toothpaste. I can get to every surface of her teeth in less than a minute. She actually loves to get her teeth brushed now. I didn't like the brush because I couldn't feel what I was brushing. And by the way, the very best toothpaste is CET poultry flavored enzymatic."

No matter how much dental care you can perform at home, always have the dog's mouth examined annually in the vet's office. Exams not only help to keep the teeth and gums healthy, they create an opportunity to check for the presence of other problems, including cancerous growths.

Photo Credit: Kristin Pollington of Milky Paws

The Matter of Genetic Abnormalities

Cavapoos can suffer from health conditions passed down from both Poodles and Cavaliers. The chances of a Cavapoo developing a health condition depend on the health of the parent.

Listed below are some of the most common conditions affecting both Cavaliers and Poodles. You shouldn't let these conditions put you off buying a Cavapoo because every dog, including purebreds, can suffer from health problems, but it's important to be aware of them and take steps to reduce the risk of buying an unhealthy puppy.

Conditions Common to Cavalier King Charles Spaniels

Syringomyelia

Syringomyelia (SM) is a condition affecting the spinal cord. It can affect any dog but is more common amongst Cavaliers. Cavaliers also develop the condition at a younger age than other breeds.

The back of a Cavalier's skull is often too small for its brain, which causes a blockage to the spinal column. This prevents spinal fluid from flowing into the spinal cord, resulting in cavities at the top of the spine.

The most common symptom of SM is scratching around the neck, which is often referred to as "air scratching." This symptom usually doesn't develop until the puppy is around six months old, which can make diagnosis difficult. As the condition develops, SM causes pain around the neck that becomes progressively worse.

SM is an extremely serious condition. There aren't many treatment options, although medication can help to manage the pain. Surgery to remove the blockage and allow spinal fluid to flow properly can sometimes stop the disease progression but is expensive and can only be performed by specialists. The condition may start to get worse even after successful surgery, as scar tissue can form leading to a new blockage.

Mitral Valve Disease

Mitral valve disease (MVD) is a condition that affects the heart. It is the most common cause of death amongst

Cavaliers around the world. Mitral valve disease is a genetic condition that affects nearly all Cavaliers by the age of ten. MVD causes one of the valves in the heart to stop working properly. This causes blood to flow in the wrong direction through the heart. Eventually, the valve stops working completely, causing heart failure.

Symptoms of mitral valve disease usually progress slowly, although the speed of progression can vary. If mitral valve disease is detected, the dog should have regular checkups to monitor how the condition is progressing.

There is no cure for mitral valve disease. Drugs can often slow the deterioration of the heart valve, but these only work in the short term. The drugs used for mitral valve disease can also cause serious side effects.

Mitral valve disease is a big problem for Cavalier breeders. A recently designed protocol states that Cavaliers shouldn't be bred until they are at least five years old, which is something to keep in mind when choosing a Cavapoo breeder. This is so that the breeder can be sure the Cavalier isn't going to develop MVD early in life.

Eye Conditions

Until recently it was common for Cavaliers to suffer from a variety of eye conditions including juvenile and congenital cataracts. These are now less common, due to breeders testing their dogs before breeding them. It's still important to ask a breeder about the condition when choosing a Cavapoo.

Conditions Common to Toy and Miniature Poodles

Addison's Disease

Addison's disease is caused by a lack of adrenal hormones. This can cause serious symptoms and is a common condition amongst Poodles.

The initial symptoms of Addison's disease can be difficult to spot. A dog may appear lethargic and find it difficult to cope with stress. These symptoms are commonly misdiagnosed, as a range of problems can cause them.

Addison's is a serious condition, but it can usually be managed successfully. A dog with Addison's disease can be given medication to reduce the effects of the condition. If the condition is not diagnosed correctly, however, it can eventually cause death.

Hip Dysplasia

A dog with hip dysplasia has an abnormally formed hip socket. The socket doesn't fit the bone correctly, which means that the joint can move around when in use. This leads to faster degeneration of the cartilage in the hip joint. Hip dysplasia is a genetic condition, but it can also be made worse by certain activities.

Hip dysplasia causes pain from a young age, and the dog may grow up thinking the pain is "normal." This means that hip dysplasia often isn't diagnosed until the condition starts to get worse, as this is when the dog's behavior begins to change.

The most common symptoms of hip dysplasia are difficulty standing up, pain when walking and an inability to stand on the back legs. Dogs with hip dysplasia also find it difficult to go up stairs and will often suddenly stop and sit on walks.

While hip dysplasia can't be cured, there are a number of treatments to reduce pain and improve the dog's quality of life. Some of the most effective include controlling the dog's weight, limiting exercise to safe activities and taking pain management medication. Supplements containing glucosamine can also be effective. Surgery, either to repair the hip joint or to replace it, is usually only recommended in severe cases and when other treatment options have failed.

Photo Credit: Helen Wilson owner of Ralph

Luxating Patella

Luxating patella is a common condition affecting small dogs. The condition occurs because the groove that holds the kneecap is too shallow or incorrectly formed causing the kneecap to come out of the groove, which prevents the leg from bending.

The most common symptom of a luxating patella is if a dog suddenly stops an activity, often with a yelp, and holds his or her leg straight. After a few minutes the leg usually returns to normal. This delay is because it takes time for the muscles around the knee to relax enough for the kneecap to re-enter the patella groove.

If a luxating patella isn't treated, it will often get worse. This can lead to pain and early-onset arthritis. Medication cannot solve the problem, so surgery is often the only option. The suitability of surgery depends on the severity of the condition. Not every dog with a luxating patella requires surgery.

Epilepsy

Epilepsy is a brain condition that causes seizures and is often passed from parent to offspring. Poodles are more prone to epilepsy than most other breeds.

The primary symptom of canine epilepsy is seizures that last up to 90 seconds. Epileptic seizures can cause the dog to fall over, bark, urinate or tense its muscles. After a seizure, the dog may appear to be confused or hungry, and may not fully return to normal for up to 24 hours.

Treatment involves medication to control seizures. Your vet will monitor drug levels in the dog's blood to ensure that the right amount is being prescribed.

Canine Arthritis

Canine arthritis, like that in humans, is a debilitating degeneration of the joints. The cartilage breaks down leading to bone-on-bone friction. This creates considerable pain and a restricted range of motion.

Treatments for dogs are the same as those used with humans. Aspirin addresses pain and inflammation, while supplements like glucosamine may be used to improve joint health. Environmental aids, including doggy stairs and ramps, remove some of the pressure on the affected joints and help pets to stay active.

Most cases of arthritis are a natural consequence of aging that require management focusing on pain relief and facilitating ease of motion.

Some dogs become so crippled their humans buy mobility carts for them. These devices, which attach to the hips, put your pooch on wheels. So long as your pet is otherwise healthy, this is a reasonable approach to a debilitating but not fatal ailment. The carts are adjustable, but when possible should be custom fit to ensure maximum mobility.

Allergies

Dogs can suffer from allergies just like humans. Anything that can touch the skin, be inhaled or eaten has the potential to trigger an adverse reaction. Owners may first realize something is wrong if the dog begins to scratch or lick excessively, or in some cases to chew or bite the paws, tail, stomach or hind legs.

In instances of airborne allergies, the dog may sneeze, cough or experience watering eyes. Food allergies often trigger vomiting or diarrhea. Skin irritations may include rashes or hives. In short, your Cavapoo can be absolutely miserable. Negative reactions in the spring or fall can likely be traced to seasonal pollen. Fleas are often the culprits in warm weather. Food allergies can occur at any time, with the greatest offenders including beef, corn, wheat, soybeans and dairy products.

Allergy testing offers a definitive diagnosis and points toward environmental and dietary changes. The tests are expensive, costing $200+ / £120+. The dog may need medication or interventions like cool, soothing baths. In cases of food allergies, special diets are common.

Plastic food bowls can cause an acne-like inflammation on your dog's chin. Switch to stainless steel, glass or ceramic dishes. Wash your pet's face with cool, clear water. If the rash doesn't begin to clear up, ask the vet for an antibiotic cream.

Summary of Cavapoo Health Problems

There are a number of health conditions that can affect Cavapoos. It's important to be aware of the most common conditions so that you can recognize the symptoms as early as possible. In addition, it's a good idea to insure a Cavapoo puppy while the dog is still young and healthy. It's never possible to predict whether health conditions are going to occur, and insuring a puppy is often cheaper than waiting for health problems to develop.

You shouldn't listen to a breeder who guarantees that their Cavapoo puppies are healthy. It's simply not possible to make this guarantee, as any hybrid dog can inherit genetic problems from parents. If a breeder isn't honest about the potential health problems associated with a Cavapoo, this is a warning that you shouldn't buy from them.

Chapter 8 – Cavapoo and Old Age

It can be heartbreaking to watch your beloved pet grow older. He may develop health problems like arthritis, and he simply might not be as active as he once was.

Unfortunately, aging is a natural part of life that cannot be avoided. All you can do is learn how to provide for your Cavapoo's needs as he ages so you can keep him with you for as long as possible.

Photo Credit: Rebecca Posten of Riverside Puppies

What to Expect

Aging is a natural part of life for both humans and dogs. Sadly, dogs reach the end of their lives sooner than most humans do.

Once your Cavapoo reaches the age of 8 years or so, he can be considered a "senior" dog.

At this point, you may need to start feeding him a dog food specially formulated for older dogs, and you may need to take some other precautions as well.

In order to properly care for your Cavapoo as he ages, you might find it helpful to know what to expect. On this page, you will find a list of things to look for as your Cavapoo dog starts to get older:

• Your dog may be less active than he was in his youth – he will likely still enjoy walks, but he may not last as long as he once did, and he might take it at a slower pace.

• Your Cavapoo's joints may start to give him trouble – check for signs of swelling and stiffness and consult your veterinarian with any problems.

• Your dog may sleep more than he once did – this is natural sign of aging, but it can also be a symptom of a health problem, so consult your vet if your dog's sleeping becomes excessive.

• Your dog may have a greater tendency to gain weight -- carefully monitor his diet to keep him from becoming obese in his old age.

• Your dog may have trouble walking or jumping --- keep an eye on your Cavapoo if he has difficulty jumping, or if he starts dragging his back feet.

• Your dog's vision may no longer be as sharp as it once was -- he may be predisposed to these problems.

• You may need to trim your Cavapoo's nails more frequently if he doesn't spend as much time outside as he once did when he was younger.

• Your dog may be more sensitive to extreme heat and cold-- make sure he has a comfortable place to lie down both inside and outside.

• Your dog will develop gray hair around the face and muzzle – this may be less noticeable in Cavapoos with a lighter coat.

While many of the signs mentioned above are natural side effects of aging, they can also be symptoms of serious health conditions.

If your dog develops any of these problems suddenly, consult your veterinarian immediately.

Caring for an Older Cavapoo

When your Cavapoo gets older, he may require different care than he did when he was younger.

The more you know about what to expect as your Cavapoo ages, the better equipped you will be to provide him with the care he needs to remain healthy and mobile.

Here are some tips for caring for your Cavapoo dog as he

ages:

• Schedule routine annual visits with your veterinarian to make sure your Cavapoo is in good condition.

• Consider switching to a dog food that is specially formulated for senior dogs – a food that is too high in calories may cause your dog to gain weight.

• Supplement your dog's diet with DHA and EPA fatty acids to help prevent joint stiffness and arthritis.

• Brush your Cavapoo's teeth regularly to prevent periodontal diseases, which are fairly common in older dogs.

• Continue to exercise your dog on a regular basis – he may not be able to move as quickly, but you still need to keep him active to maintain joint and muscle health.

• Provide your Cavapoo with soft bedding on which to sleep – the hard floor may aggravate his joints and worsen arthritis.

• Use ramps to get your dog into the car and onto the bed, if he is allowed, because he may no longer be able to jump.

• Consider putting down carpet or rugs on hard floors – slippery hardwood or tile flooring can be very problematic for arthritic dogs.

In addition to taking some of the precautions listed above in caring for your elderly Cavapoo, you may want to familiarize yourself with some of the health conditions your dog is likely to develop in his old age.

Elderly dogs are also likely to exhibit certain changes in

behavior, including:

- Confusion or disorientation
- Increased irritability
- Decreased responsiveness to commands
- Increase in vocalization (barking, whining, etc.)
- Heightened reaction to sound
- Increased aggression or protectiveness
- Changes in sleep habits
- Increase in house soiling accidents

As he ages, these tendencies may increase – he may also become more protective of you around strangers.

As your Cavapoo gets older, you may find that he responds to your commands even less frequently than he used to.

Photo Credit: Nicki Mannix owner of Bella

The most important thing you can do for your senior dog is to schedule regular visits with your veterinarian. You should also, however, keep an eye out for signs of disease as your dog ages.

The following are common signs of disease in elderly dogs:

- Decreased appetite
- Increased thirst and urination
- Difficulty urinating/constipation
- Blood in the urine
- Difficulty breathing/coughing
- Vomiting or diarrhea
- Poor coat condition

If you notice your elderly Cavapoo exhibiting any of these symptoms, you would be wise to seek veterinary care for your dog as soon as possible.

Euthanasia

The hardest decision any pet owner makes is helping a suffering animal to pass easily and humanely. I have been in this position, and even though I know my beloved companied died peacefully and with no pain, my own anguish was considerable. Thankfully, I was in the care of and accepting the advice and counsel of exceptional veterinary professionals.

This is the crucial component in the decision to euthanize an animal. For your own peace of mind, you must know that you have been given the best medical advice possible.

My vet was not only knowledgeable and patient, but she was kind and forthright. I valued all of those qualities and hope you are as blessed as I was in the same situation.

The bottom line is this: No one is in a position to judge you.

You must make the best decision that you can for your pet and for yourself. So long as you are acting from a position of love, respect and responsibility, whatever you do is "right."

Grieving a Lost Pet

Some humans have difficulty fully recognizing the terrible grief involved in losing a beloved canine friend.

There will be many who do not understand the close bond we humans can have with our dogs, which is often unlike any we have with our human counterparts.

Your friends may give you pitying looks and try to cheer you up, but if they have never experienced the loss of such a special connection themselves, they may also secretly think you are making too much fuss over "just a dog."

For some of us humans, the loss of a beloved dog is so painful that we decide never to share our lives with another, because the thought of going through the pain of such a loss is unbearable.

Expect to feel terribly sad, tearful and yes, depressed, because those who are close to their canine companions will feel their loss no less acutely than the loss of a human friend or life partner.

The grieving process can take some time from which to recover, and some of us never totally do.

After the loss of a family dog, first you need to take care of yourself by making certain that you remember to eat regular meals and get enough sleep, even though you will feel an almost eerie sense of loneliness.

Losing a beloved dog is a shock to the system that can also affect your concentration and your ability to find joy or be interested in participating in other activities that are a normal part of your daily life.

Other dogs, cats and pets in the home will also be grieving the loss of a companion and may display this by acting depressed, being off their food or showing little interest in play or games.

Therefore, you need to help guide your other pets through this grieving process by keeping them busy and interested, taking them for extra walks and finding ways to spend more time with them.

Waiting Long Enough

Many people do not wait long enough before attempting to replace a lost pet and will immediately go to the local shelter and rescue a deserving dog. While this may help to distract you from your grieving process, this is not really fair to the new fur member of your family.

Bringing a new pet into a home that is depressed and grieving, may create behavioral problems for the new dog that will be faced with learning all about their new home, while also dealing with the unstable energy of the grieving family.

A better scenario would be to allow yourself the time to properly grieve by waiting a minimum of one month to allow yourself and your family to feel happier and more stable before deciding upon sharing your home with another dog.

Managing Health Care Costs

Thanks to advances in veterinary science, our pets now receive viable and effective treatments. The estimated annual cost for a medium-sized dog, including health care, is $650 / £387. (This does not include emergency care, advanced procedures or consultations with specialists.)

The growing interest in pet insurance to help defray these costs is understandable. You can buy a policy covering accidents, illness, and hereditary and chronic conditions for $25 / £16.25 per month. Benefit caps and deductibles vary by company. To get rate quotes, investigate the following companies in the United States and the UK:

United States

http://www.24PetWatch.com
http://www.ASPCAPetInsurance.com
http://www.EmbracePetInsurance.com
http://www.PetsBest.com
http://www.PetInsurance.com

United Kingdom

http://www.Animalfriends.org.uk
http://www.Healthy-pets.co.uk
http://www.Petplan.co.uk

Cavapoo owner Louise Driscoll adds: "Some companies will receive the bill from the vet upfront so the client doesn't need to claim. It saves a scary/unexpected bill and hours trying to claim back the money. I'd strongly advise taking out a pet plan."

Bonus Chapter 1 - Interview With Kirstin Pollington

Can you tell us who you are and where you are based?

My name is Kirstin Pollington. I am a mum of one to my daughter Jasmine, a wife to my husband Danny. We live in a tranquil and picturesque part of Devon, England. We are surrounded by beautiful countryside, with some fantastic walks over our own ground and around the neighbouring fields.

I am the founder of Milkypaws which I established in 2010. Before Milkypaws I was a hobby breeder of Cavaliers as this breed was my childhood dog and I fell in love with their temperament. That was until I was holidaying in Florida USA when I noticed the beautiful and most charming Cavapoo. From then on I was hit by the Cavapoo "bug" and I then found myself falling in love with every Cavapoo and Cockapoo I see. "Sometimes I feel like a crazy lady who has to stop to cuddle every doodle I meet". It was then I decided to breed my own litter of Cavapoos and I never looked back.

How did you become a dog breeder?

Back in 2007 my husband Danny was a long distance HGV driver and was away from home for weeks at a time. This I found was a very lonely time for me. So I decided I would add Jo and Kissy to our family. My very own Cavalier sisters. They are so beautiful and were perfect in every way. After a few years when Kissy was of age and after consulting with our vet and my mother-in-laws who bred Cocker Spaniels at the time, I decide that I would let Kissy become a mum and we had 5 very cute puppies, 1 little girl and 4 little boys. I loved having the puppies around the place and I knew it would be hard parting with them so I decided to keep one, the only girl. Missy I decided to call her and she was then my third Cavalier.

Another few years passed and I wanted to change our lifestyle from town to country. It took a lot of persuading, but my husband finally agreed and we sold up to move rural. It was then I found another passion in horses and Cocker Spaniels. After embracing the country that we now call home, I dug and researched anything and everything possible in regards to breeding healthy puppies, it was then I decided to found Milkypaws.

How did you first come across Cavapoos?

In 2009 whilst on holiday in Florida, we were searching around to find a post box and we found ourselves at the lovely area called Celebration. It has a lovely green patch with a beautiful lake and everyone was out walking their dogs. Me being me decided to stroll around this lake and to watch the dogs playing and running about. It was then I could see walking closer, a dog that resembled a Cavalier but has a gorgeous long, fluffy and wavy coat. I knew I had to stop and ask its owner to find out about his dog. It was a Cavapoo and I was smitten. I was so smitten that the rest of our holiday became my research ground to find out more about this beautiful mix.

Do you know much about the history of the Cavapoo in the UK?

There isn't much history about the Cavapoo in the UK as they are relatively new. Although they are now becoming popular in the UK, Cavapoos were developed to be low shedding which is ideal for people who suffer from allergies who are looking for a family pet. Their colouring and size all depends on their parents. Being able to get a Cavapoo in different sizes means that they attract more families. F1 Cavapoos are delightful dogs to have around the family home and are certainly becoming popular not just in the UK but in other countries too.

Is there much awareness of the Cavapoo in the UK and do people recognize them in the street?

There still isn't much awareness of Cavapoos in the UK and as there are so many doodle crosses being bred now it can be hard to distinguish between them all. However I am having a lot of phone calls regarding Cavapoos just from people seeing one while on a walk. So their beautiful and gracious look are attracting more people so I don't think it will be too long before they are well known. Since my first litter of Cavapoos to now, I would say that they certainly more recognisable. If people haven't seen one they have heard about them.

What types of people are buying Cavapoos and why?

I tend to find that people who are purchasing a Cavapoo are either first time dog owners or retired people who are looking for a quiet natured and easily manageable pet. They have the ability to learn and are not highly energetic. As their coat is low-shedding they are still extremely popular with people who suffer with allergies and for people who want a fur free home.

Is it possible to describe a fairly typical Cavapoo?

Cavapoos are generally charming as both their parents' breeds are loving, playful and outgoing. They are highly trainable although it has been known for a Cavapoo to prefer to sit on your lap for the warmth and attention, rather than performing for you, but I am sure a treat will help persuade them. They are not the best guard dog but I am certain they will greet visitor and intruders with their tail wagging.

Cavapoos can easily adapt to most lifestyles, they have a medium activity level and will play well with young children and also they like chill out time and a cuddle on the sofa. They will need a good walk a day or a good playtime at home. Temperaments can be affected by inheritance and their environment. If you begin training and socialization early you will be rewarded by a loyal and loving companion.

The Cavapoo look can vary and it is down to inheritance. They are bred in lots of different colours and sizes. The average Cavapoo's height is between 13-18 inches from the floor to their shoulder, they generally weigh in at 5-10 kg and their coat is wavy and shaggy. Their life span is between 10-15 years.

Can you offer advice to people looking to buy a Cavapoo?

I'm always happy to offer help and advice to people looking to purchase a Cavapoo puppy, as this can be a complete minefield for new owners. Try and make sure the timing is going to be right to welcome the new puppy into your household, as well as a member of the family being able to look after your new puppy if you are needed to work for a few hours a day. Have a ring around your local vets and ask them to recommend any local breeders and to have a list of questions to ask the breeder before purchasing a new puppy.

Health testing is the most important thing you will need to know when searching for a puppy. Poodles need to be DNA clear for Degenerative Myelopathy / DM, Malignant Hyperthermia / MH, von Willebrand disease Type I / vWD I and Progressive Retinal Atrophy / prcd – PRA. Miniature Poodle will need to be BVA Hip scored.

Cavalier will need to be DNA tested clear for Dry Eye and Curly Coat syndrome / CCS and Episodic Falling in Cavalier King Charles Spaniel / EF.

How much should people expect to pay?

This is a hard question to answer. Generally a fully health tested Cavapoo will cost around £800-£1000 from a good breeder. I have seen adverts advertising litters for as little as £400 but then some as much as £1,200. I advise that whatever the cost you are prepared to pay, always check that health tests are done and to have met at least the mother of the litter. A little tip is to see the mother interacting with her puppies.

Are there things new owners do that perhaps frustrate you?

I get frustrated when potential owners come to me with a picture they have found online and tell me they 'want a dog exactly like that'. It can be tough. I know that Cavapoos are very pretty and their beauty is what attracts most people but I do like to consider their personality and characters. I do want new owners to have the dog they desire but each puppy in one litter has a different character and I feel this is more important as generally Cavapoos are beautiful regardless of their size or colour.

What sort of challenges do you face in mating two different breeds?

I personally take extra care at this point in deciding a match between the two dogs. My way is to ensure the safest way possible. I take the weight and height into consideration for example I would not mate a tiny Toy Poodle female with a huge, chunky Cavalier male as this would cause a lot of stress on the mum to carry big puppies. In fact I do not breed where the Poodle is the mum at all.

What is the typical temperament of a Cavapoo?

Cavapoos are very family orientated and if you treat them with respect they will respect you back. They are good companions for a young family or an elderly person with the ability to adapt to most lifestyles. They are extremely loyal, loving and sociable making them the great family pet. They are super affectionate making them a good snuggle pet.

Do you have any special feeding routines or diet?

You may find that Cavapoos can be fussy when it comes to eating. I strongly advise that you stick to a crunchy kibble rather than tinned meat, as this will help with keeping their teeth clean. Cavapoos are extremely keen for a treat or ten, so you will need to watch their diet to stop them becoming overweight. I also recommend feeding them in a routine always feeding at the same time, twice every day. Sticking to the same food will help to stop them being fussy and to stop tummy upset, which could occur if you were to feed them different food each time.

What colors and sizes are most popular?

Cavapoos can come in a variety of colours, but I find that the Apricot or Ruby colours are most popular. They are extremely sought after if they have a white flash on their face. If is wonderful when a litter of puppies arrive as you never know what colour they are going to be. Also as the puppy matures into an adult the colour may change, so you can't really tell their true colour until they are fully grown.

The colour can change drastically if they are clipped before they are fully grown. Try to avoid clipping them right before they are an adult. I generally keep mine complete knot free by regular brushing and just trim them around their eyes, mouth and bottom. Once they are old enough I will have them clipped shorter. This I find will keep their colour looking vibrant.

What health issues do Cavapoos tend to suffer from?

Genetic DNA health testing is important in Cavapoo's. We need to minimise the occurrence of the diseases now and in the future of our puppies.

Toy Poodle

- Degenerative Myelopathy / DM
- Malignant Hyperthermia / MH
- von Willebrand disease Type I / vWD I
- Progressive Retinal Atrophy / prcd – PRA

Miniature Poodle

- Progressive Retinal Atrophy / prcd – PRA.
- Degenerative Myelopathy / DM
- Malignant Hyperthermia / MH
- von Willebrand disease Type I / vWD I
- BVA Hip Score.

Cavalier King Charles Spaniel

- Dry Eye and Curly Coat syndrome / CCS
- Episodic Falling in Cavalier King Charles Spaniel / EF

Apart from DNA testing of the parents, the puppies should also be seen by a vet so they can listen to their hearts, check their mouth, ears and other parts of their body.

Are there any tips you would like to share with new owners?

When searching for a puppy, speak to more than one breeder, view more than one litter. Make sure you see at least the mother interacting with her puppies. Take time to read the health tests in detail and don't be afraid to ask questions that you may have. Remember that a puppy is a big commitment, make sure you are ready. Puppies are sweet and cute and those puppy dog eyes are going to melt your heart. Just please do your research on them before you decide.

The new owner should be fully educated in terms of training a puppy. Read as much as possible or attend training classes with your puppy. You need to know yourself that you are training your dog correctly, be firm but fair. Dogs do need boundaries but also a lot of rewarding.

Raising a puppy is very much like raising your first child, there is just so much to learn and quickly, but the biggest thing to remember is to relax and enjoy every moment of it.

Kirstin Pollington of Milky Paws
http://www.milkypaws.co.uk

Bonus Chapter 2 - Interview With Rebecca Posten

Rebecca thanks for doing this interview, can you tell us who you are and where you are based?

Riverside Puppies is located in Crocker, Missouri.

How long have you been involved in breeding Cavapoos and what made you get started?

I have been raising Cavapoos for 10 years.

Photo Credit: Rebecca Posten of Riverside Puppies

Is the Cavapoo becoming more popular or less as time goes on, perhaps your thoughts on how you see the breed progressing?

It is becoming extremely popular. We currently have a 12-14 month wait for our puppies.

What type of owners are buying Cavapoos and what are they looking for?

People that love Cavaliers, but don't want to deal with health issues or shedding. Cavapoos are also a great family dog and many of our pups are used as therapy dogs. They do well with children (assuming the child is taught how to interact the correct way) and other pets.

Can you offer advice to people looking to buy a Cavapoo?

Make sure they have the space (they do like a nice walk or romp in the yard) and time for a new pet.

Are there things that you see owners doing that frustrate you?

Generally it has to do with potty training. The pups are given too much unsupervised time in the home or given treats or scraps.

What would be the positives and negatives of owning a Cavapoo?

Pros: This is a smart, athletic and fun breed. They are easy to train and love to please their owners. They are low to non-shedding, making them ideal for families with allergies. They enjoy the water.

Cons: As with all pets they require time and training. Their coat must be brushed often, to keep it from matting. It is a good idea to have them groomed 3-4 times each year. Due to their long, floppy ears they are prone to ear infections.

What feeding routines and types of food/supplements do

you recommend?

We feed Nutrisource twice daily. There should be no need for supplements, if your dog is at a healthy weight and getting plenty of exercise. Rawhides and Nylabones to keep gums and teeth healthy.

Are there accessories that you can particularly recommend owners buy?

We like Snuggle pup products, Exerhides and Nylabones.

Are there health issues owners should be aware of?

Mitral Valve Heart Disease (mainly in F2 breedings), Luxating Patella

Rebecca Posten of Riverside Puppies
http://www.riversidepuppies.biz

Bonus Chapter 3 - Interview With Nicki Mannix

We find out about Cavapoos in Australia from owner Nicki Mannix. The Cavapoo is known as a Cavoodle in Australia.

Nicki, how long have you been a Cavapoo owner and what made you choose a Cavapoo?

I've been a Cavapoo owner for 4 years now, I didn't set out to get a Cavapoo but spotted Bella on an online rescue site and it was love at first sight, she was 18 months old at the time and her original owner had passed away. I didn't realise at the time how lucky I was to be getting such a fabulous dog that is so sought after here in Australia.

How much did Bella cost to buy and where did you buy her?

Being a rescue I was required to only pay a couple of hundred dollars. I've since realised Cavapoos sell here for anything up to $1400 US.

Do you have any advice to potential new buyers/owners?

I've learnt a lot through the online community in the last few years about the importance of choosing the right breeder - someone who not only provides well balanced healthy puppies but who also does the right thing by the parents of your new dog.

Cavapoos are part of the family and thrive on human companionship so if you are not home much, don't have time to care for them and plan to have an outside dog, Cavapoo's aren't for you.

Has Bella had any health issues?

I've been very lucky with Bella she has had no major health concern. We struggled a bit to get her diet right for the first couple of years, Cavapoos have sensitive tummies and she also had some anxiety issues in the early days that didn't help her tummy problems.

Why do you think people should choose the Cavapoo over another breed of dog?

Cavapoos are the most loving loyal intelligent dogs I have come across... not to mention the cuteness factor.

What would you say are common mistakes that you have seen Cavapoo owners make?

I think with a lot of new dog owners, people underestimate the time and expense of having a dog. Cavapoos don't require huge amounts of exercise but they do need a daily walk and some play time, you also need to put in the effort early on to build the bond and set the boundaries. I worked with a trainer who came to the house and to be honest it was really me that needed the training not Bella, she caught on really fast once I knew what I was doing.

Vet bills are expensive, add in grooming, food, flea and tick treatment and I think people get a shock at the commitment required to be a responsible dog owner.

What are your feeding routines such as how often and what types of food do you feed Bella?

Bella has 2 meals a day, I've found she thrives on the BARF raw food diet. She has the occasional bone or chicken neck, raw of course, and has some natural chicken jerky as a treat of a night.

I'm very strict with her diet she has never eaten my food while I'm eating and as a result isn't a dog who hangs around for scraps at our meal times.

Can you offer any grooming tips, advice and perhaps some accessories that you wouldn't be without?

Bella has an appointment at the groomers every 6 weeks as much as I love her hair all long it takes a lot of work to keep it matt free, this way I only need to brush her once a week as opposed to every day when its longer. In winter she is washed once in-between by me but twice in the summer, it can be very hot where we live and she is well and truly an indoor girl so I like to keep her nice and clean.

A good quality shampoo and conditioner designed for dogs is a must. I'm very lucky she is a bit of a princess and walks around mud and puddles not liking to get her feet wet and dirty, I notice at the dog park she is quite unique in this way.

Are there some tips and advice that you think most owners would be unaware of?

I'm in a Facebook Cavapoo group and the one thing most seem to be taken by surprise by and have in common is separation anxiety. Bella is lucky, she mostly has someone with her, I notice a lot of owners end up getting a second dog for companionship and always a Cavapoo - once you have had one it is hard to look at any other breed.

Are there any final thoughts that you wish to share?

If you do decide on a Cavapoo be prepared to be loved like no dog has ever loved you before, you will be followed around, have no privacy and no time on your own, but with a bit of work will have a loyal loving companion and life will never be the same again.

Thank you Nicki for providing this interview for our readers.

Glossary

Abdomen – The surface area of a dog's body lying between the chest and the hindquarters also referred to as the belly.

Allergy – An abnormally sensitive reaction to substances including pollens, foods, or microorganisms. May be present in humans or animals with similar symptoms including, but not limited to, sneezing, itching, and skin rashes.

Anal Glands – Glands located on either side of a dog's anus used to mark territory. May become blocked and require treatment by a veterinarian.

Arm – On a dog, the region between the shoulder and the elbow is referred to as the arm or the upper arm.

Artificial Insemination – The process by which semen is artificially introduced into the reproductive tract of a female dog for the purposes of a planned pregnancy.

Back – That portion of a dog's body that extends from the withers (or shoulder) to the croup (approximately the area where the back flows into the tail).

Backyard Breeder – Any person engaged in the casual breeding of purebred dogs with no regard to genetic quality or consideration of the breed standard is referred to as a backyard breeder.

Bitch – The appropriate term for a female dog.

Blooded – An accepted reference to a pedigreed dog.

Breed – A line or race of dogs selected and cultivated by man from a common gene pool to achieve and maintain a characteristic appearance and function.

Breed Standard – A written "picture" of a perfect specimen of a given breed in terms of appearance, movement, and behavior as formulated by a parent organization, for example, the American Kennel Club or in Great Britain, The Kennel Club.

Brows – The contours of the frontal bone that form ridges above a dog's eyes.

Buttocks – The hips or rump of a dog.

Castrate – The process of removing a male dog's testicles.

Chest – That portion of a dog's trunk or body encased by the ribs.

Coat – The hair covering a dog. Most breeds have both an outer coat and an undercoat.

Come Into Season – The point at which a female dog becomes fertile for purposes of mating.

Congenital – Any quality, particularly an abnormality, present at birth.

Crate – Any portable container used to house a dog for transport or provided to a dog in the home as a "den."

Crossbred – Dogs are said to be crossbred when each of their parents is of a different breed.

Dam – A term for the female parent.

Dew Claw – The dew claw is an extra claw on the inside of the leg. It is a rudimentary fifth toe.

Euthanize – The act of relieving the suffering of a terminally ill animal by inducing a humane death, typically with an overdose of anesthesia.

Fancier – Any person with an exceptional interest in purebred dogs and the shows where they are exhibited.

Groom – To make a dog's coat neat by brushing, combing or trimming.

Harness - A cloth or leather strap shaped to fit the shoulders and chest of a dog with a ring at the top for attaching a lead. An alternative to using a collar.

Haunch Bones – Terminology for the hip bones of a dog.

Haw – The membrane inside the corner of a dog's eye known as the third eyelid.

Head – The cranium and muzzle of a dog.

Hip Dysplasia – A condition in dogs due to a malformation of the hip resulting in painful and limited movement of varying degrees.

Hindquarters – The back portion of a dog's body including the pelvis, thighs, hocks and paws.

Hock – Bones on the hind leg of a dog that form the joint between the second thigh and the metatarsus. Known as the dog's true heel.

Inbreeding – When two dogs of the same breed that are closely related mate.

Lead – Any strap, cord, or chain used to restrain or lead a dog. Typically attached to a collar or harness. Also called a leash.

Litter – The puppy or puppies from a single birth or "whelping."

Muzzle – That portion of a dog's head lying in front of the eyes and consisting of the nasal bone, nostrils, and jaws.

Neuter – To castrate or spay a dog thus rendering them incapable of reproducing.

Pedigree - The written record of a pedigreed dog's genealogy. Should extend to three or more generations.

Puppy – Any dog of less than 12 months of age.

Separation Anxiety – The anxiety and stress suffered by a dog left alone for any period of time.

Sire – The accepted term for the male parent.

Spay – The surgery to remove a female dog's ovaries to prevent conception.

Whelping – Term for the act of giving birth to puppies.

Withers – The highest point of a dog's shoulders.

Wrinkle – Any folding and loose skin on the forehead and foreface of a dog.

Index